RHS

GREENER GARDENING

Vegetables

RHS

GREENER GARDENING

Vegetables

The Sustainable Guide to Growing Planet-friendly Crops

Sally Nex

MITCHELL BEAZLEY

RHS Greener Gardening: Vegetables
Author: Sally Nex
First published in Great Britain in 2024
by Mitchell Beazley, an imprint of Octopus Publishing Group Ltd,
Carmelite House, 50 Victoria Embankment, London EC4Y 0DZ

www.octopusbooks.co.uk
An Hachette UK Company
www.hachette.co.uk

Published in association with the
Royal Horticultural Society

ISBN: 978-1-78472-930-1

A CIP record of this book is available from the British Library

Printed and bound in China

Mitchell Beazley Publisher: Alison Starling
Mitchell Beazley Editorial Assistant: Ellen Sleath
RHS Publisher: Helen Griffin
RHS Consultant Editor: Simon Maughan
RHS Head of Editorial: Tom Howard

Conceived, designed and produced by
The Bright Press,
an imprint of The Quarto Group.
1 Triptych Place, London, SE1 9SH
(0)20 7700 9000
www.Quarto.com

Publisher: James Evans
Art Director: James Lawrence
Editorial Director: Isheeta Mustafi/Anna Southgate
Managing Editor: Jacqui Sayers
Editor: Emily Angus
Project Editor: Rica Dearman
Design: Clare Barber/Studio Noel
Illustrations: Sarah Skeate
Picture Researcher: Tom Broadbent/Katie Greenwood/Emily Angus

The Royal Horticultural Society is the UK's leading gardening charity dedicated to advancing horticulture and promoting good gardening. Its charitable work includes providing expert advice and information in print, online and at its five major gardens and annual shows, training gardeners of every age, creating hands-on opportunities for children to grow plants and sharing research into plants, wildlife, wellbeing and environmental issues affecting gardeners.

For more information visit www.rhs.org.uk
or call 020 3176 5800.

FSC
www.fsc.org
MIX
Paper | Supporting responsible forestry
FSC® C016973

Contents

Introduction

When you're pottering about in your backyard planting beans and peas or cutting some lettuce for your tea, it doesn't exactly feel like the cutting edge of climate activism.

But growing your own food can change the world.

Growing a few vegetables is something we can all do, even with minimal resources, to help bring down carbon emissions and tackle the scourge of climate change. Every sprig of broccoli you pick, every carrot you pull is one you haven't had to buy from the shops, so it's ultra-low carbon food.

Households that grow their own fruit and vegetables are three-and-a-half times more likely to eat their recommended five portions of fresh food a day. They also eat about 40 per cent more fruit and vegetables overall – so, if you grow your own food, you naturally tend to eat a healthier, more plant-based diet. You feel good – and your carbon footprint falls still further.

But you can only unleash the full climate-busting potential of your vegetable patch when you garden in a green way, too.

Grow your food hand in hand with nature and you get natural pest control, from ladybirds to blackbirds. Put away the spade and lavish your soil with organic mulches and your thriving soil biosphere plugs your plants into a rich seam of subterranean nutrients and moisture.

Your garden already has pretty much everything you need: greenery for homemade fertilizers, autumn leaves for potting-compost-grade leaf mould and seeds to start off next year's crops. The more you rely on natural, renewable resources, the less you have to buy, and the lower your environmental impact.

This book is your guide to setting up a green vegetable garden. In Part 1 you'll find all you need to know about setting up your growing area; in Part 2 we'll run through the techniques you need to get up and growing; and Part 3 takes you through how to grow crops for every season of the year.

Follow the techniques on these pages and you, too, can make a personal contribution towards the global effort to tackle climate change and help nature back from the brink.

GO GREENER

One in three people in the UK grows at least some of their own food, filling gardens, containers or window boxes with vegetables, salads, fruit and herbs.

Setting up a new vegetable garden

Here you are at last, gazing at the patch of land that will be your new vegetable garden. A whole world of possibility stretches out ahead of you, full of organic, fresh, mouthwateringly tasty vegetables, and all grown as sustainably as possible – so they're good for both you and the planet. Now you're here, you just want to plunge in and get planting! But stop, just for a moment. Rush at your new plot without knowing what the soil's like, or where the shady corners are, and you'll likely end up with unhappy plants and a disappointing harvest. Get to know the land, plan your first steps carefully and you can design the vegetable plot of your dreams, where you and your plants can grow and thrive together, each season better than the one before.

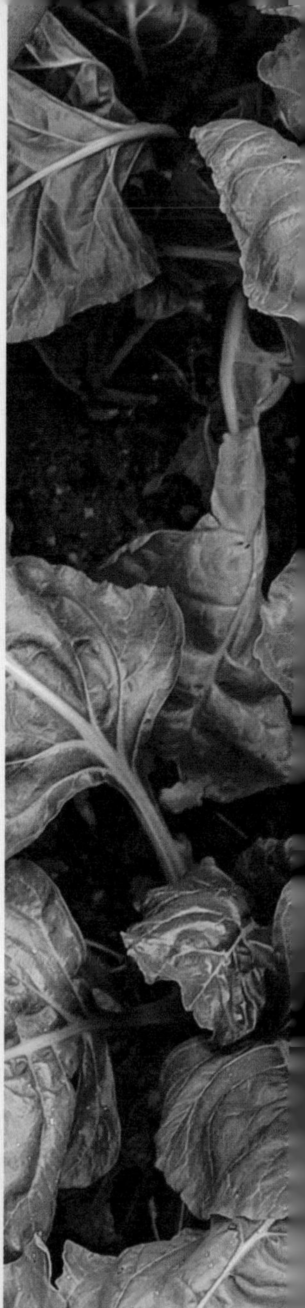

Choosing where to site a new vegetable garden

The dream vegetable plot is one that's in full sun yet sheltered from the worst weather. It'll have deep, well-cultivated, rich but moisture-retentive soil, without any perennial weeds. And no slugs. Or rabbits, come to that...

Wouldn't that be nice! In practice, choosing the best spot for your vegetables is all about weighing up the pros and cons and picking the area with the fewest drawbacks.

Sunshine is top of the list of must-haves – you can do something about most other problems, but not lack of light. Most types of fruit, vegetables and herbs thrive in full sun, so the most successful vegetable plots bask in at least six hours of sunshine a day in midsummer.

That said, a few shady spots are invaluable for leafy vegetables and most salads, which can bolt (run to seed) when they're too hot and dry. And many vegetables, including roots, potatoes and brassicas such as cabbages, cope well with just three to six hours of sunlight in summer – so even slightly shadier gardens can produce a good range of fresh food.

Your dream vegetable plot

Here are some tips for a happy, healthy and eco-friendly vegetable garden...

A little shade alongside fences, hedges or sheds keeps leafy salads and vegetables happy

Use bricks, timber or stone to create contained borders or level terraces on a sloping site

CHOOSING THE PERFECT SPOT

DO

- Check there are no noxious weeds on site, such as Japanese knotweed.
- Get to know your soil (see page 14) - the RHS offers a testing service to members.
- Dig a 30cm-deep (12in) hole to test drainage: water should soak away within a few hours.

DON'T

- Pick a spot in deep shade, with less than three hours of sunlight a day.
- Site your vegetable garden on a very steep slope - though gentle inclines are fine.
- Put your vegetable garden near large trees or right next to thick hedges – they can cast shade and suck moisture and nutrients from the soil.
- Plant in areas under water in winter.

GO GREENER

An edible shelter belt can be created by a row of Jerusalem artichokes or blackcurrant bushes, planted on the windward side of the plot.

A hedge filters the wind to a gentle breeze, providing shelter from weather

Line gates with rabbit-proof wire mesh, so they can't squeeze through

Some shelter is essential – most plants struggle in the teeth of a gale, so if your would-be plot is in a windy spot, plant a hedge or put up a wattle fence made of hazel to filter the wind.

A gentle slope is no problem, but anything steeper will need terracing to create flat areas on which to garden. A wall or fence at the bottom of a slope will trap frost, so any vegetable plot sited here will take longer to warm up in spring, and blossom and young growth could be damaged. Trees also suck moisture and nutrients from the ground, so avoid planting under their canopy.

Don't be put off by weeds – even brambles and annoying perennials such as bindweed can be conquered with persistence. But do allow space for rainwater harvesting (see page 76) and composting; and perhaps a shed or tool store, so you're all set and ready to go.

Getting to know your soil

The earth in which your plants grow underpins everything you do – get your soil right, and everything else follows. Get to know your soil before you start, and you have the blueprint for a successful vegetable patch.

Take a generous fistful of damp soil, inspect it closely, then give it a squeeze and try to roll it into a ball. This simple test tells you lots about what's under your feet. It is also worth finding out the pH of your soil by using a simple test kit, the colour chart for which can be seen opposite.

If it's easily moulded Your soil is mainly clay – it'll usually (but not always) be neutral to acidic, heavy and poorly drained. Potatoes, peas and fruit typically grow well in clay soils, which retain nutrients well. Improve clay soils by adding plenty of organic matter (see page 56).

If it falls apart easily when you try to mould it You have sandy or silty soil – neutral to acidic, easy to work, but drought-prone. Suitable for most vegetables, just add plenty of organic matter to enhance the soil's ability to hold on to water and nutrients.

If it's greyish and falls apart easily You are gardening on chalk. Like sand, it's light and free draining, but is stony with thin topsoil. Brassicas love it, but potatoes are prone to scab and carrots fork easily. Again, adding organic matter helps add bulk to chalky soil.

CLAY SOIL

SANDY SOIL

CHALKY SOIL

Soil in new-build houses

Gardens in newly built houses often have compacted, thin or rubble-filled soil, offering little goodness for plants' roots. You can still have a vegetable patch – it just takes a bit more work.

- Fork over the area lightly and remove what rubble you can.
- Build raised beds, at least 20cm (8in) high, on top.
- Fill with a 50:50 mix of bought-in topsoil and homemade garden compost, municipal green waste or well-rotted farmyard manure.
- Allow to settle for a few days, top up if necessary and your new vegetable beds are ready to plant!

The best garden soil is rich in humus – natural organic debris such as dead leaves, which boosts your soil's ecosystem and helps your plants grow. High levels of humus turn any soil dark brown, almost black, and wriggling with life. So, feed your soil and you'll feed your plants, too: build humus levels by mulching with organic matter (see page 63) to create a rich, deep, fertile topsoil your vegetable plants will love.

GO GREENER

One teaspoon of healthy garden soil contains about a billion microorganisms, many of which help your plants grow better.

pH scale

Mildly acidic pH 6–6.8 is the ideal pH for vegetable growing, with its optimum nutrient availability.

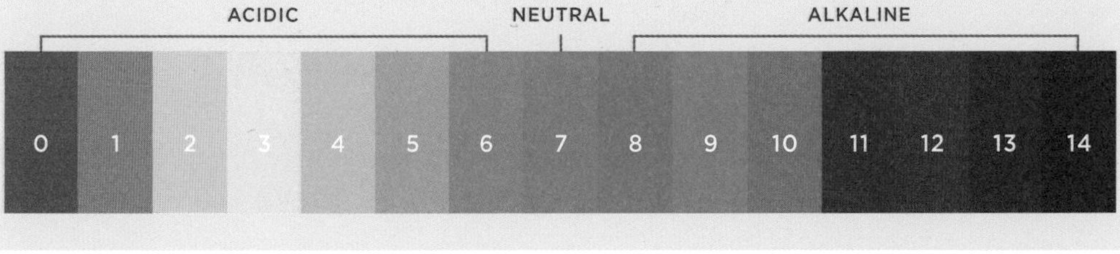

Equipment: what you'll need

Kitting out your shed with all the tools you'll need to look after your new patch can seem daunting: one glance at the tool section in your local garden centre tells you there's a bewildering array of gadgets for every possible task.

In fact, the list of must-have equipment for the first year in your new patch is quite short. You can always add to your tool collection later, but for now, just half a dozen essentials are all you need.

Essentials

Border spade Border spades save your back as the smaller blade means lighter loads. The standard shaft length is 70cm (28in), but there are longer and shorter models to suit your height and strength.

Garden rake A garden rake, with short tines, spreads mulches; lawn rakes, with longer, fanned tines, collect fallen leaves for leaf mould.

Hoe You'll be hoeing off annual weeds weekly in summer – a D-shaped Dutch hoe is a good all-rounder, while golf-club-shaped swoes let you hoe closer to plants.

Hand fork Essential kit for light weeding tasks. Short-handled forks are good for most jobs; those with long handles save you bending down as much.

Trowel You can plant everything from potatoes to peas with a pointed hand trowel. Some are usefully marked with planting distances on the blade.

Watering can Galvanized steel watering cans last many years – buying second-hand is greener – and you'll need a medium rose for general-purpose use.

Nice to have

Secateurs Only really needed if you're growing and pruning fruit trees and bushes.

Wheelbarrow A medium capacity of 70–90L is a useful size: solid tyres avoid punctures.

Bucket or trug For collecting weeds and holding your harvest.

Mattock For clearing rough ground and tough, woody weeds such as brambles.

OPTIONAL EXTRA TOOLS

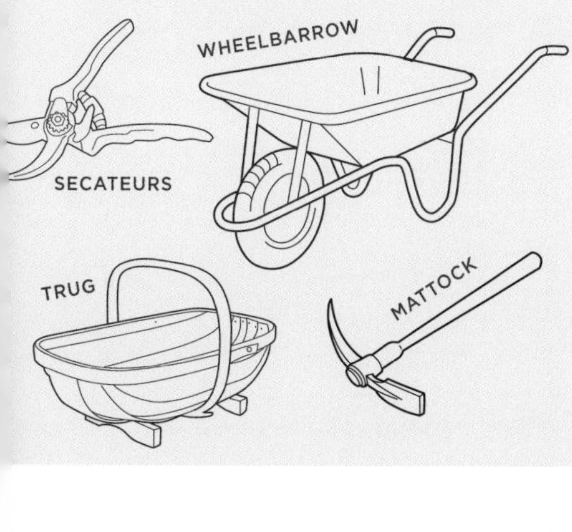

What to wear

There's no such thing as bad weather, just the wrong clothing, so they say – and good-quality gardening gear keeps you dry, comfortable and safe.

Gloves Hard-wearing gardening gloves will protect your hands from thorns.

Boots Good-quality wellies or well-made, supportive hiking boots keep you outside for hours. If possible, buy second-hand.

Hat Keep rain and sun off your face with a close-fitting, wide-brimmed gardening hat.

Equipment: greener gardening tools

New garden tools can be resource-hungry to manufacture, with a high carbon footprint (especially if they're imported), so buy wisely to reduce their impact on the environment.

Gardening gadgets seem like a good idea at the time, but they almost always end up as forgotten shed clutter. So, buy only what you're sure you will use, and invest in the highest-quality tools you can – the best last a lifetime.

Buying tools second-hand saves resources, energy and packaging. Find reconditioned tools on sale from vintage specialists or on online auction sites; you can pick up second-hand wheelbarrows, watering cans, galvanized buckets and other gardening gear for a song at auction houses.

If you do want to buy new, try to weigh up the environmental costs. It's not always a straightforward choice. Buy wood and metal tools to avoid contributing to plastic pollution, and they'll often last longer (you can also repair them if they break). But manufacturing new items from steel carries a very high carbon footprint. Metal wheelbarrows often also come coated in rust-resistant epoxy – a type of plastic. You can buy wheelbarrows made of 100 per cent recycled plastic – but even recycled plastic ends up in landfill eventually.

Best of all are handcrafted items made as close to where you live as possible, from sustainable materials such as locally coppiced chestnut, ash or oak. Hand-forged spades and forks from traditional tool companies, Sussex trugs and wooden garden sieves bought from local craftspeople leave little trace on the environment, last for years – and they're things of beauty you'll love forever.

Take good care of your tools, keeping them clean and well oiled in the shed over winter, and they'll last much longer.

TIP

To prolong the life of your tools, apply linseed oil to both the wood and metal parts, using an old rag. Then polish off the excess with another clean cloth.

Looking after your tools

Look after your tools with love and they last years – saving the planet's resources and your money.

- Clean mud and sap off tools after every use.
- Sharpen the blades of secateurs, spades and hoes.
- Sand wooden handles smooth, and wipe with linseed oil to keep them supple.

Power tools

Hand tools have the lowest environmental impact, but sometimes power tools are more practical. Battery-powered mowers, hedge trimmers and strimmers are now as powerful as petrol tools and kinder to the environment (though issues remain over the impact of lithium mined for lithium-ion batteries). For smaller gardens, use corded electric power tools powered with renewable electricity, if possible, as they are greenest of all. In tests, petrol-powered leaf blowers, hedge trimmers and strimmers give off more pollution than is legally permitted for cars.

The low-carbon greenhouse

A greenhouse is every gardener's dream – it's your special place where you can garden even when it's raining, and tend mouthwatering summer crops such as tomatoes and peppers or out-of-season winter salads.

Build your own greenhouse

Recycled windows make wonderfully quirky, eco-friendly greenhouses.

1. Collect second-hand wooden windows and doors from online marketplaces, auctions or skips (with permission).
2. Lay the windows out flat to work out how they'll fit together, leaving as few gaps as possible. Use this as a template to build wooden stud walls from good-quality, sturdy 5 x 10cm (2 x 4in) wood, creating a frame for each window.
3. Sink 10 x 10cm (4 x 4in) fenceposts into the ground at each corner.
4. Fix the stud walls securely to the vertical posts.
5. Screw windows firmly in place onto their individual frames and attach the door with hinges.

6. Add the roof – a lean-to design, with the front slightly higher than the back, is simplest. Build another wooden frame and use more windows if they're suitably lightweight; or attach second-hand sheets of lightweight, transparent, corrugated plastic instead (these can be recycled once they reach the end of their useful life).
7. Block any gaps with wood, then use non-toxic exterior caulk to seal windows and frames.

New greenhouses have a high carbon footprint, especially aluminium models; wooden frames, especially naturally long-lasting cedar, are greener, though need regular maintenance. They're also eye-wateringly expensive.

Second-hand greenhouses, on the other hand, neatly sidestep the need to use any more of the Earth's resources and you won't have to remortgage the house either. Find unwanted greenhouses on online marketplaces, buy-nothing sites such as Freecycle and advertised in local newspapers.

You'll usually have to dismantle them yourself – take photos before disassembling, and use masking tape to label each section. Place cardboard between glass to protect it during transport.

Once home, level your site and add a foundation. Your greenhouse may already have a metal base, which you can set straight onto compacted ground. If not, build a low wall of second-hand bricks or lay repurposed paving slabs, using sustainable concrete substitute. Fix the frame securely on top, bolt everything together and finally clip in the glass.

TIP

Always wear eye protection and gloves, and handle glass and old wood with care.

Running a low-carbon greenhouse

Once you've got hold of your greenhouse, it'll quickly become the engine room of your garden. A well-run greenhouse is never empty, from the first seeds sown in spring to the last winter salads.

Greenhouses are also artificial growing environments, and any plants you grow in them require more by way of resources, from pots and water to feed. Add heating and your greenhouse habit begins to look increasingly unsustainable.

It doesn't have to be like that. Set your greenhouse up from the start for minimum impact on the environment and you can still enjoy growing under glass without the guilt.

Seasonal tasks

Spring – Raising seedlings Wait until mid- to late spring to sow, and avoid high-energy heated propagators by germinating seeds inside your already heated house. Move trays into the greenhouse when seedlings appear. Late winter to early/mid-spring sowings can be stored indoors for the same reason.

Summer – Greenhouse crops Plant into greenhouse borders if you can, or use second-hand terracotta containers and hessian growbags (see opposite) rather than plastic. Water by hand using harvested rainwater, and feed weekly with homemade comfrey tea (see page 73).

Make your own hessian growbags

Hessian growbags are cheap, plastic-free and ideal for raising tomatoes, cucumbers or melons – just throw them onto the compost heap at the end of the season.

1. Buy hessian coffee or potato sacks second-hand from online auction sites.
2. Sew the ends shut with jute garden twine.
3. Use scissors to cut through the top layer of the sack, opening it up across the middle to make two large planting pockets like a saddlebag.
4. Fill these with peat-free compost and they're ready to plant!

Autumn – Refill with salads Sow hardy winter salads and leafy greens such as mizuna, pak choi and land cress into biodegradable or resuable pots or containers outdoors in late summer. By the time you're clearing away the tomatoes and cucumbers, they'll be sturdy young plants ready for refilling borders and containers or for harvesting then and there.

Winter – Overwintering tender plants Keep frost-sensitive herbs such as lemon verbena going into a second season by potting them up before winter to bring into the greenhouse where it's a few degrees warmer. You shouldn't need to heat the greenhouse; keep plants very dry, line the walls with cardboard, and wrap individual plants with hessian and straw through cold snaps.

Using your space wisely

A well-designed vegetable patch makes everything about your gardening life easier. Plan a space that's beautiful yet practical and you'll end up with a plot that works well for you and your vegetables.

First, measure out your garden to scale and draw up a proper plan. Start with a working area where you can have sheds, greenhouses and cold frames within easy reach of each other. Build in sustainability from the start with a sturdy set of compost bins (see page 54), plus rainwater-harvesting tanks to collect water from every roof.

Next, draw in a main path leading directly from the entrance to the work area. Negotiating narrow, wiggly paths with a fully laden barrow quickly loses its charm, so make it as straight and wide as you can. A width of 60–90cm (23–35in) lets a wheelbarrow through comfortably.

Then, set out your vegetable beds. Raised beds help define concentrated growing spaces where you can target mulches and group similar plants together, making it easier to look after them.

The ideal width for a vegetable bed is 1.2m (4ft), which allows you to reach into the middle from the path without having to tread on the soil.

They can be any shape – get creative and arrange rectangles and L-shapes in simple geometric patterns for a handsome potager-style garden.

Raised beds help define your space and they help you target water and mulches exactly where they are needed.

GO GREENER

Rather than replacing existing paving slabs, lift stones and re-lay them; fill in between with second-hand bricks or old roof tiles laid on their ends, or plant gaps with creeping herbs.

Which path?

Woodchip This beautifully natural-looking option is fully sustainable and cheap. Persuade a local tree surgeon to drop some off and lay it at least 10cm (4in) thick. Tread down well and top it up every year.

Paving slabs Re-use second-hand slabs for a lower carbon footprint and lay on a 10cm bed of compacted sand.

Gravel Source carefully, as gravel is sometimes dredged from the seabed. Pea shingle tends to find its way off the path and into your vegetable beds, so self-binding gravel is usually a better option – it sets hard, so is more practical, and it's a by-product from quarrying, so is more sustainable, too. Crushed brick – a by-product of the construction industry – is another option.

Grass paths These harbour slugs and need regular maintenance, usually with high-energy power tools.

Growing vegetables in small spaces

When space is tight, there often isn't room for a dedicated vegetable plot. But even in small gardens you can still grow plenty of fresh food – you just need a few clever techniques.

Growing vegetables in small spaces needs different rules. When space is tight, there's no room for traditional rows or space-hogging vegetables such as potatoes, onions or Brussels sprouts; concentrate instead on vegetables that give you the highest yields for the smallest space, such as climbing French beans, chard and cut-and-come-again lettuce. And if you want to grow larger crops, choose compact patio varieties such as 'Patio Star' courgettes and 'Hestia' runner beans.

Grow things differently, too – sow new potatoes in sacks to save space in the garden, and edge flowerbeds with a froth of curly green parsley, or red and green cut-and-come-again lettuces. Walls, fences and the sides of sheds double your vegetable-growing potential. Train apple, pear and cherry trees into fans and espaliers, and grow climbing vegetables from runner beans and mangetouts to crookneck squash over trellises to enjoy gorgeous flowers followed by handsome fruits – and a great harvest.

Expand your growing space

Once you've got the vegetable-growing bug, you just want to grow more, so try these strategies for getting your hands on more garden space:

Allotments Local councils look after most allotments, though some are run by private organizations. Don't be put off by a waiting list – you'll often get to the top faster than you think.

Garden shares Put a shout-out on social media or download garden-sharing apps such as AllotMe to find neglected gardens waiting for someone to look after them.

Community gardens Charities growing for food banks and care homes welcome volunteers in return for a share of the food.

Sustainability and small plots

Vertical gardens Make your own by fixing second-hand guttering to a wall at 30cm (12in) intervals, or attach large, recycled food containers securely to strong wire mesh on timber battens.

Green roofs Herbs or alpine strawberries love the free-draining conditions on a shed roof. Check the structure can take the weight before adding a roof garden using reclaimed wood and crushed cockleshells (rather than high-carbon perlite) for drainage.

Square foot gardening Divide up vegetable beds into smaller patches (at least 30cm^2/1ft^2) using short lengths of hazel and string, then sow a different vegetable into each.

Making a start on your vegetable garden

Once you've picked out the perfect spot for your vegetable patch and drawn up a plan, you'll be itching to get growing. But it pays to take your time and get things right from the start.

It's easy to get disheartened if you spend the whole of your first season whacking brambles or building paths without harvesting so much as a bean. So, break down the task into stages, and tackle one small area at a time.

Get just one bed up and running, and plant it with simple, easy-to-grow vegetables such as runner beans, potatoes and beetroot. Look after them well and you'll be growing and harvesting your own homegrown food in your very first season.

Cut back any brambles and dig out the roots.

In between tending your crops, start gradually making your plans come to life, installing sheds, building compost bins and laying paths.

Keep the rest of the plot neat while you're getting around to bringing it into the main vegetable garden – but cut down on the time you spend maintaining it as much as possible.

Mow turf – but only once a month (use a strimmer or mower set to a high cut), to allow nectar-rich buttercups, dandelions and clover to flower for pollinating insects. If you're taking on an overgrown plot, scythe or strim back everything, then cover with cardboard held in place with old bricks or stones. Woody weeds such as brambles and tree seedlings should be dug out by the root if possible.

This holds back regrowth for about a season, after which you'll need to re-cover with more cardboard. Each year, strip back the cardboard from the next area you want to bring back to life.

ECO WORRIER

1kg (2.2lb) of fruit or vegetables accounts for about 0.8kg (1.8lb) of greenhouse gases (less if it's homegrown) – compared to about 10kg (22lb) per kilo for pork or chicken, and over 70kg (154lb) for beef.

When to make a new vegetable garden

The ground is easiest to work in spring and autumn when the weather is fairly kind. But there's no bad time to start growing vegetables – just change the crops you sow to suit.

➊ **Spring** Sow hardy crops from peas and lettuces to beetroot and broad beans.

➋ **Summer** Sun-loving dwarf French beans, mangetouts and sweetcorn can be sown as late as midsummer.

➌ **Autumn** Concentrate on cool-weather oriental salads such as mizuna, winter lettuces, corn salad and land cress.

➍ **Winter** Even in winter you can start growing – plant garlic cloves, and overwinter hardy broad beans for early crops next year.

Setting up new vegetable beds

Building new vegetable beds on top of the soil involves very little digging – and that's good news for your back and the planet.

Whenever you turn over the earth, you release the carbon it contains, and disrupt the delicate subsoil ecosystem. Leave well alone and simply build your bed on top, though, and your plants plug into a web of mycorrhizal fungi and beneficial bacteria.

This soil sample shows the rich layers that develop in 'no-dig' gardens.

TIP

Building vegetable beds on top of the ground leaves the soil beneath undisturbed and keeps he carbon it holds locked away.

Creating no-dig beds at ground level

1. Scalp turf to ground level with a mower and remove weeds with a hoe. The only digging you'll need to do is cutting out woody roots such as bramble or dock using a mattock or deep spade.
2. Next, lay thick layers of cardboard across the area, damping it down before treading it flat to the ground. This is enough to kill off turf altogether – it will also stop perennial weeds such as bindweed coming through for much of the season, giving you a year of mostly weed-free growing.
3. Then, top the whole thing off with a mulch of organic matter, 5–15cm (2–6in) deep, depending on how much you have available. Homemade garden compost is ideal, but you can also use municipal green waste from your local council, or very well-rotted farmyard manure. Plant seedlings and young plants straight into the mulch and they simply grow down through the cardboard into the soil beneath. Unwanted seedlings will germinate in the mulch, but are easily pulled out by hand as they appear.

Constructing a raised bed

If you want a smarter look, raised beds are handsome and help define your vegetable-growing areas – they'll hold mulches in place more efficiently, too. Sides should be at least 15cm (6in) high.

1. Scalp turf and weeds as per 1. opposite, and roughly level the area.
2. Cut reclaimed scaffold boards to length; and make four pegs out of 5 x 5cm (2 x 2in) timber about 10cm (4in) longer than the width of the boards. Cut one end at an angle to make a point.
3. Nail the scaffold boards securely to the pegs to make a box.
4. Use a mallet to tap the pegs into the ground until your bed sits level and snug against the earth.
5. Line the base with thick cardboard, wet it and tread flush to the ground. Fill your bed with a 50:50 mix of compost and topsoil, topping off with a 5cm mulch of organic matter.

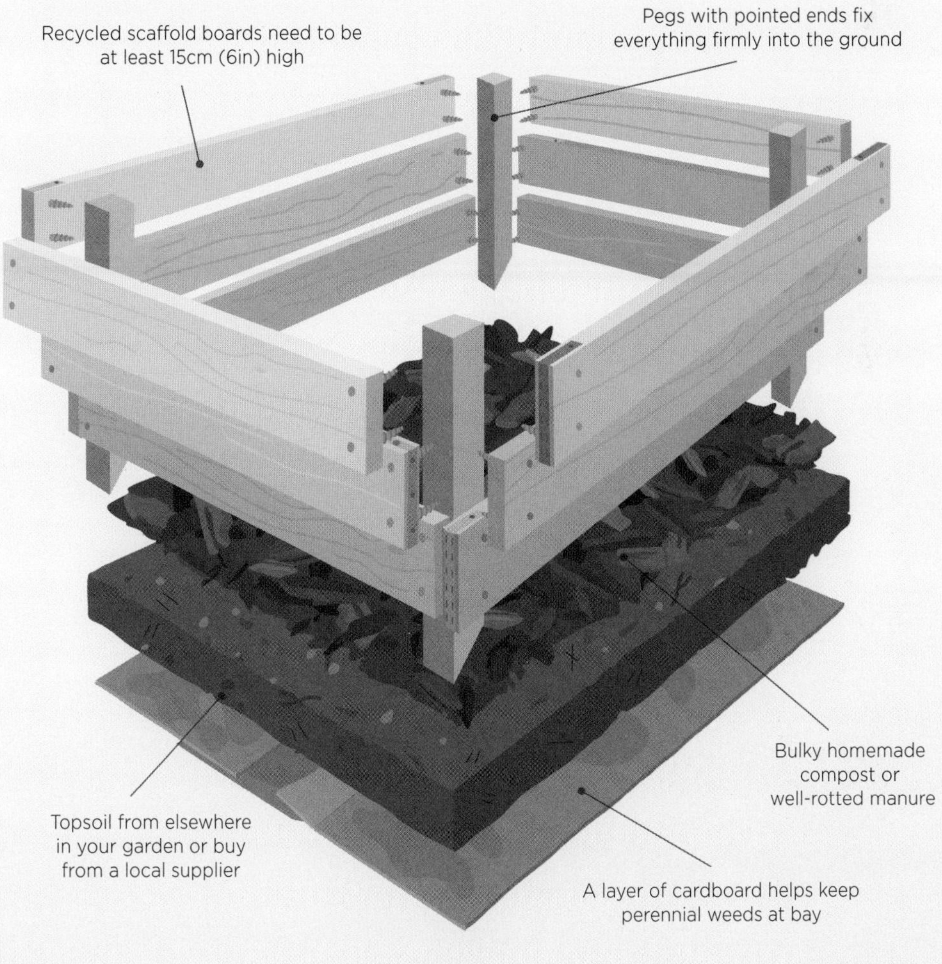

Choosing which vegetables to grow

Now for the exciting bit! The fruit, vegetables and herbs you choose to fill your new garden with are what it's all about – the promise of delicious, freshly picked, organic, sustainably produced food.

You tend not to waste food you've grown yourself, simply because you know exactly how much work goes into producing it, and you're proud of every leaf you pick. When you've spent weeks tending to their every need, you don't throw out your carrots just because they're wonky – after all, they'll still taste great!

Even so, choose what you grow carefully and plant only what you're sure you will eat. You might be tempted to grow courgettes, for example, because everyone else does and you've heard they're prolifically generous. But if nobody in your family likes courgettes, most of your harvest will end up on the compost heap. Better to put your time, effort and garden space towards growing something you all enjoy: French beans, perhaps, or broccoli.

So, pause before you plunge in, and draw up a list of fruit and vegetables your family loves. Make plenty of room for real favourites, so there's lots to go round; and add seasonal treats such as sweetcorn and asparagus, or pumpkins for Halloween.

Start your garden with easy, reliable and generous vegetables first – those that don't require much mollycoddling and suffer few unwanted insects or diseases. Then, once you've mastered these, you can move on to fussier crops such as Florence fennel, cauliflowers or spinach, which have very particular requirements and need a little more experience to grow successfully.

Get the kids involved with the family vegetable patch from the start and you'll sow the seeds for a lifetime of healthy eating.

Five vegetables for beginners

Potatoes Plant after the last frosts and they simply grow; new ('first early') and second early varieties are all but bombproof.

Radishes Ideal for super-fast harvests, seeds germinate within days and you'll be pulling roots within six to eight weeks.

Baby-leaf salads Perfect for containers; grown fast and picked young, there's no time for insects to bother them.

Chard Lush, nutritious greens just like spinach but much easier, as they're drought tolerant and take a little neglect.

Beetroot Large, easy-to-handle seeds you can sow direct; harvest young, at ping-pong ball size, and they're ready within eight weeks.

What variety to choose

Browse the seed racks in any garden centre and you'll find a bewildering choice of varieties, each growing a little differently – some are tall, some are short, some grow better in containers or mature more quickly so they're ready to harvest sooner.

Before you make your selection, do your research so you know what to expect. Big maincrop 'Alderman' peas, for example, can hit 2m (7ft) by the time they're mature, so need big, sturdy supports capable of holding the weight of a fully grown plant and its pods. But fast-maturing 'Meteor' peas grow to about 45cm (18in) tall with a relatively small harvest. It is possible to grow them without support; otherwise use a few twigs to keep them upright.

There are plenty of clues on seed packets and in catalogues that tell you more about how your variety will grow, too.

Dwarf/patio/container These make small plants with compact root systems designed for container life. You'll still get a good harvest, and there are dwarf varieties for almost every type of vegetable nowadays, although it may take a bit of experimentation to discover which ones grow as advertised and produce the best crops for you.

Early/mid-season/late Early crops are first to give you a harvest, while late or maincrop varieties mature more slowly. Early varieties guarantee results in colder regions with short growing seasons; you can also plant two or three varieties with different maturing times to spread your harvest over a longer period.

Disease resistant Varieties with a natural ability to resist some of the more common diseases such as blight or scab are invaluable for sustainable growers, as they stay healthy without the need for chemical pesticides.

Heirloom/heritage These lovely old varieties are said to major in flavour, though they're sometimes less reliable to grow than modern hybrids. Many Victorian heirlooms, though, such as 'Imperial Green Longpod' broad beans, have never been bettered.

You may find that red lettuce varieties such as 'Red Salad Bowl' or 'Dazzle' are slightly less prone to slug and snail damage, because of their higher levels of anthocyanin.

TIP

AGM stands for Award of Garden Merit, and means the variety, such as this 'Golden Sunrise' tomato, has come out top in extensive RHS trials, so it's likely to be among the best available, with a good reliable harvest.

Achieving self-sufficiency

Many vegetable growers dream of becoming self-sufficient – that wonderful moment when you realize you're supplying all your daily fruit, vegetables and herbs from your back garden and you can't remember the last time you stopped by the fresh produce aisle in the supermarket.

How to make it work

Self-sufficiency is a great goal to have. Food accounts for about a third of your carbon footprint, so by producing all your fresh food yourself, you slash your environmental impact. When every pea you pick makes you burst with pride, you'll also be more likely to eat your five a day – this is healthier for you, and since it encourages a more plant-based, low-carbon diet, it is better for the planet, too.

For full self-sufficiency in fruit, vegetables and herbs, you need a fair amount of space. Allotments are a standard 250m^2 (2,690ft^2) because that's considered to be enough land to feed a family of four year-round – though it helps if you have more, especially if you like potatoes.

Rather than going the whole hog, though, it's more manageable to think of self-sufficiency in particular types of vegetable. So, you could start by deciding you're going to grow all your own salads from now on; then next year, you could try becoming self-sufficient in herbs or leafy greens. That's the kind of self-sufficiency you can achieve, whatever the size of your growing space – even if all you have is a few spacious containers.

What's for tea? Picking supper from the garden means you eat more seasonally, and that's better for you and the planet.

Self-sufficiency easy hits

Take your first steps towards self-sufficiency and cross these vegetables off your shopping list right from the start:

Baby-leaf salads Sow three roomy (35–45cm; 14–18in) containers one month apart, harvest each in turn, then resow as soon as you finish picking for a continuous supply.

Evergreen herbs Rosemary, common thyme, sage and bay stay green and pickable year-round; plant in a sunny spot in the ground or in containers.

Spinachy greens Grow bombproof chard or perpetual spinach year-round (see page 111); add summer spinach for its finer flavour.

Kale Grow a different variety for each season (see page 110) or just grow a succession of baby leaves year-round in pots or in the ground.

Squash Eat courgettes, patty pans and crookneck squash fresh through summer, then grow good keepers such as 'Crown Prince' for winter eating.

Self-sufficiency strategies

The more fresh food you grow, the more self-sufficient you'll be, so make sure you use every inch of your plot. Keep it working hard right through each season, so you harvest as much produce as your garden can grow.

Aim to refill vegetable beds at least once or twice through the season, planning ahead so you have the next crop ready and waiting the moment the previous one is harvested.

After you've cleared the winter brassicas in spring, for example, replant straight away with young bean seedlings sown a few weeks earlier into saved toilet rolls, so the land is back in production right away. Once new potatoes are cleared, replant with courgettes or sweetcorn – again, raised in pots and ready to plant.

You can keep planting well beyond summer, too – sow winter salads into pots in a cold frame in midsummer and simply drop them into your vegetable beds as they empty, to keep them pumping out produce right through until spring.

Don't be afraid to double up in your vegetable beds. Grow shade-loving spinach or beetroot between brassicas, tuck cut-and-come-again lettuces or moss parsley around the edges, and plant wigwams of climbing beans among squash plants. Like all legumes, beans 'fix' nitrogen from the air, providing natural fertilizer; in return, those big, lush squash leaves keep out weeds and lock in moisture.

Self-sufficiency doesn't mean everything is always available. In fact, one of the joys of becoming self-sufficient is rediscovering the excitement of seasonal eating. Keep a steady supply of store cupboard staples such as salad, leafy greens, kale and herbs going all year-round (see page 106), but add highlights such as spring asparagus, summer mangetout peas and strawberries, and autumn pumpkins. The arrival of each treat becomes a big event, to be looked forward to and celebrated – you'll never see food in quite the same way again.

Grow several different varieties of vegetables in roomy containers and keep the harvest coming by simply replanting with new crops as gaps open up.

Planting relay races

Try these combinations to keep your vegetable beds full for as much of the year as possible.

	Spring	Summer	Autumn
Bed 1	New potatoes	Sweetcorn and squash (*sown into saved toilet rolls*)	Winter salads (*sown in pots in late summer*)
Bed 2	Broad beans (*overwintered*)	Calabrese (*raised in pots*) underplanted with spinach	Chicory (*sown in pots in summer*) and moss-curled parsley
Bed 3	Baby carrots, sown direct Early beetroot under cloches	Tomatoes (*raised in pots*) French marigolds	Garlic (*to overwinter*)
Bed 4	Spring cabbage	French beans (*sown into saved toilet rolls*)	Onions (*to overwinter*)

Building on your first year

Congratulations! You've made it through your first season. Now you've had a taste of the delights of freshly picked, homegrown food, as well as the life-affirming joy of spending time outside getting close to nature, you'll just want to build on your success.

As your first year draws to a close, take stock and look back – while it's still fresh in your mind – at what's gone well and what hasn't been so successful. A notebook or garden journal app is invaluable for jotting down thoughts and snatches of inspiration.

You've probably got lots of exciting ideas for expanding your vegetable-growing empire, but it's still wise to pace yourself. Remove the cardboard from the next section of your plot, but only as much as you're sure you have time to tend. The rest can wait for another year. The old cardboard can be added to the compost heap.

Draw up a planting plan for your second season – incorporating your newly opened area – and jot down which crops you want to grow where, making sure you aren't growing the same crop in the same place as last year (see page 80 for more on crop rotation). And if you noticed a lull in your harvest this year, include crops at their best at that time of year, so you don't go short again.

GO GREENER

Make space for wildlife, even in a vegetable plot - leave a corner undisturbed, build a log pile or make a pond and the creatures that move in will help control unwanted critters, too.

Crops for your second year

You'll want to repeat crops that did well for you – but now you've got a year's experience under your belt, challenge yourself with fussier crops, expand your horizons with unusual choices and invest in the future with long-lasting perennials.

Cauliflowers You can grow cauliflowers year-round, but summer cauliflowers are easiest. Don't let them dry out, and keep growing conditions absolutely consistent.

Florence fennel Like cauliflowers, aniseed-flavoured Florence fennel won't tolerate setbacks. Wait until early summer to sow, and keep well-watered.

Asparagus When you plant asparagus, you know you're in it for the long haul, as it'll still be pumping out succulent, sweet spears 20 years from now (see page 120).

Perennial kale Perennial crops are a must-have for sustainable vegetable gardeners – harvest season after season of free food while helping your soil's ecosystem thrive (see page 108).

Yacon One of a range of relatively new crops on the block, yam-like yacon roots are sweet enough to eat raw. Other fun, unusual crops worth trying include oca, okra and tomatillos.

Taking it to the next level

After a few seasons of learning from your successes and (even more so) mistakes, you'll feel more sure of yourself and ready to take on new challenges.

Take your vegetable growing to the next level and you can fine-tune seed sowing, add to your repertoire and garden even greener.

Nursery bed Make a small, raised bed in a sunny spot and sow winter brassicas direct, in short rows. Thin seedlings to 10cm (4in) spacings and once they're about 15cm (6in) tall, transplant to their final growing space. Nursery beds are easier to protect from critters, and greener than raising seedlings under cover, as you don't need compost, pots or a greenhouse.

Fruit No kitchen garden is complete without a good range of fruit – plant a berry patch of raspberries, gooseberries, redcurrants and blackcurrants, and train fruit trees against walls and fences in fans and espaliers.

Cloches Use long row covers to warm the soil before early sowing and protect leafy salads into winter. Buy second-hand barn-style cloches and fit them with toughened glass – they're expensive, but last longer than polythene tunnels, and they're recyclable, too.

Cold frames Invaluable for hardening off seedlings in spring. Build hotboxes – 1m-deep (3ft) pits of fresh manure, turned until it heats, then topped with 10cm of compost) and cover with a cold frame to create a naturally heated tropical microclimate for heat-loving crops such as melons.

Trained fruit means you can squeeze an orchard into even tiny spaces, while cold frames are handy for hardening off seedlings.

Permaculture guilds

Permaculture is a way of growing which takes its inspiration from nature to grow food more sustainably, by using ideas like regenerative soil care, perennial crops and 'guilds' – mutually beneficial groups of plants. Team plants which help each other together, like squash, legumes and marigolds (as seen below) and they'll feed, protect and support each other. For more on permaculture, see the Resources section on page 170.

Deep green gardening

Try these low-carbon, low-impact gardening techniques to harness the power of nature and make your vegetables grow that bit greener:

Forest gardens Mimic the structure of a woodland, layering an upper storey of fruit trees with mid-level berry bushes and shade-loving perennial leafy greens at ground level for a permanently planted edible forest that's a haven for wildlife, too.

Lasagne beds Cover the soil with cardboard, then alternate layers of manure and green waste (lawn clippings, kitchen waste, etc). Top with soil, leave to rot over winter, then plant.

Hügelkultur Mound up old wood (ideally rotting), cover with half-rotted compost and top with topsoil; plant for a no-dig, high-carbon growing space rich in organic matter.

Vegetable garden techniques

Growing your own food has to be by far the most enjoyable way of lightening your footprint on the planet. Every pea and potato you eat from your back garden is one you don't have to buy from the shops – and that means food that hasn't racked up carbon emissions through intensive agriculture, transport and packaging. When you grow fruit and vegetables in your garden, all they need is a patch of good soil, plus a little care and attention from you. Armed with the sustainable techniques outlined on these pages, you can enjoy organic food raised as nature intended: no chemical pesticides, no food miles and no plastic packaging.

How to sow your seeds

However long you've been gardening, seed sowing is a rollercoaster ride. There's the long, anxious wait when nothing is happening, then the thrill as that first tiny green nub pokes through. Just remember, though, that seeds are pre-programmed to grow – so give them what they need, and you won't go far wrong!

It's all in the timing

Most seeds germinate given enough warmth, moisture and light – but avoid sowing too soon, however much you're itching to get gardening in early spring. They'll germinate happily enough, but with natural light or warmth in short supply, they'll need lots of extra help from energy-hungry heated propagators to grow lights, which are expensive, and not very green.

You'll get equally good results by waiting until mid-spring, when it's lighter and a little warmer. Sow in pots of homemade or good-quality peat-free seed compost on windowsills indoors; there's no need for propagators as most seeds germinate at 18–21°C (64–70°F), coincidentally, the temperature of the average living room! Move seedlings into a cool greenhouse or cold frame once they're up, though, so they can grow on in full daylight.

TIP

Sow carrots and parsnips directly where they're to grow, as both can fork when grown in containers. Always sow coriander direct, too, as transplanting makes it bolt.

By late spring, the soil should be warm enough to sow direct into the garden, just as nature does it. Even so, some particularly tasty seedlings, such as lettuces or beans, are likely to be munched by marauding slugs and mice the moment they pop up above the soil, so it's often a wiser use of resources to sow them in pots, so you can keep them safe. Once they're big enough to fill 10cm (4in) pots, they'll be less attractive to critters, so you can plant them out in the open garden.

Once beans grow big enough to fill a small pot they're ready to plant outside.

Sowing outdoors

- Check the soil is warm enough – if it still feels chilly to the touch, wait a little longer.
- Use a pointed trowel to make a fairly shallow channel, or drill, about 1–2cm (<1in) deep.
- If the soil is dry, water thoroughly, flooding the drill, and let it drain away.
- Sprinkle seeds sparingly along the bottom – aim to space seeds 2–5cm (0.5–2in) apart.
- Gently brush soil back over the seeds until they're just covered and firm lightly.
- Label and water them whenever the soil starts to dry out, until the seedlings emerge.

Which pots for which seeds?

So, you have your seeds ready to go – and then what? Do you reach for a seed tray, some modules or just a pot? Here's your quick guide to what to sow where.

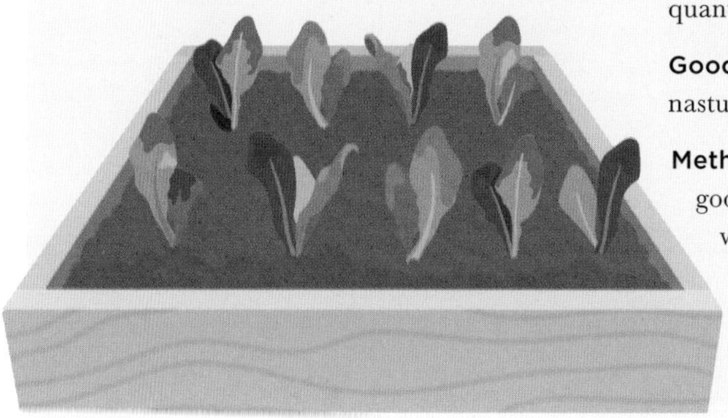

WOODEN SEED TRAY

Seed trays when you need large quantities of one type of vegetable.

Good for: lettuces, baby-leaf salads, nasturtiums, marigolds.

Method: Fill wooden seed trays with good-quality, peat-free seed compost, water and allow to drain. Scatter seeds sparingly across the surface, then sieve more compost over the top to cover.

Newspaper modules for cluster sowing and vegetables that dislike root disturbance.

Good for: beetroot, turnips, leeks, annual herbs such as parsley.

Method: Roll newspaper strips around a 5cm-diameter (2in) paper potter, fold the surplus over and crush flat to make a module. Fill with compost, water, then sow seed on top.

NEWSPAPER MODULES

Soil blocks for most vegetables with medium-sized seed.

Good for: lettuces, beetroot, brassicas, annual herbs.

Method: Make up blocking compost (one part garden soil to four parts multipurpose, peat free compost) and thoroughly wet it. Use a soil-blocking mould to make compressed blocks and sow into the top, removing the need for plastic, as the block is compact enough to stand alone.

SOIL BLOCK

CLAY POT

Clay pots for when you don't need many plants.

Good for: tall brassicas such as kale, melons, cucumbers, courgettes, squash, tomatoes.

Method: Fill 10cm (4in) pots with sieved seed or multipurpose compost, water, then space seeds evenly and cover with more compost.

Toilet roll inners for large seeds that need a deep root run.

Good for: beans, sweetcorn.

Method: Stand cardboard tubes in an old seed tray, or recycled plastic tray, lined with newspaper and fill with peat-free multipurpose compost. Water well and bury a seed in each, about 2cm (0.5in) below the surface.

TOILET ROLL INNERS

Sourcing seed sustainably

Producing packeted seed for your garden can be an international business – seeds are often developed in one country, collected in a second, then shipped to you in a third, picking up a sky-high carbon footprint along the way. Therefore, wherever possible, buy from local seed companies, which grow, collect and process seed themselves, organically and without plastic packaging. Even better – grow and collect it yourself; you can find out how on page 100.

Looking after your seedlings

Germinating your seeds is just the beginning – now you have trays and pots full of babies to nurture as they grow into sturdy young plants ready to launch into the big, wide world.

Your first job is to give them their own individual pots; seed compost only has enough nutrients to support seedlings for a short time after they've germinated. As a rule of thumb, once a seedling has its first pair of 'true' leaves (the ones that look like the adult plant), it's ready for its own pot.

Gently separate your seedlings – tip them out of the pot you sowed them in and carefully work them apart, or use a pencil or chopstick to ease them out of a seed tray or pot. Handle seedlings by their leaves only – if you break a leaf, it's not a disaster, but if you damage those delicate stems, it's game over.

Fill 5cm (2in) newspaper modules or soil blocks (for smaller seedlings, such as lettuces) or 10cm (4in) cardboard or clay pots (for larger seedlings such as courgettes or tomatoes) with homemade or peat-free multipurpose compost, and make a hole in the middle. Settle the seedling into the hole so the lowest leaves are just above compost level, then gently firm the compost back round the stem, and water.

At this point, start feeding your seedlings with half-strength liquid seaweed feed once a week. As your seedlings grow, they'll fill their new pots and roots will start appearing at the sides of newspaper and cardboard pots (if you're using clay pots, gently tip each plant out occasionally to see if the roots are filling the space yet). If it's too soon to plant them in the garden, move them again into a pot one size larger, to keep them growing until they can go outside.

Transplanting self-sown seedlings

Vegetables such as lettuces, radishes, rocket and chard, plus herbs such as parsley, dill and chervil, will sometimes self-seed naturally if you let them flower at the end of the season, giving you bonus crops sown nature's way. Look out for self-sown seedlings popping up near the parent plant, then lift them carefully with as much root as possible and replant the largest, healthiest seedlings where you want them to grow.

Hardening off and planting out

After a month or two enjoying a cushy life indoors, your vegetables will be sturdy youngsters bursting out of their pots. It's time to toughen them up and send them out into the open garden, so they can reward all your care with a bumper harvest.

Building resilience

If you plant them outside straight away, the jump from a warm, sheltered greenhouse into a relatively cold and blustery garden can be a real shock, and young, tender plants can be slow to recover. Do it gradually, over about two weeks, and your plants have time to thicken leaf structures and strengthen stems, so they're much more resilient and hardly notice the change.

Hardening off is easiest with a cold frame. Transfer your seedlings to the cold frame, then for the first few days, open the lid a crack in the day and close it at night. Gradually raise the lid a little more every few days, opening it at night, too, after the first week, until you remove it completely; your seedlings are now ready to plant.

If you don't have a cold frame, move the plants outside into a sheltered spot during the day and bring them in at night. Cover with plastic-free biodegradable PLA fleece, or simply an old white cotton bedsheet for the first few days (horticultural fleece is made of plastic, so is best avoided), then leave them uncovered during the day, still bringing them in at night. For the next few days, leave them out at night but covered; and finally, if the weather isn't too bad, leave them out uncovered at night, too.

Make your own cold frame

Cold frames are incredibly useful and are easy to make from reclaimed wood and salvaged windows.

1. Find windows from architectural salvage yards, online auctions or the neighbour's skip (with permission!).
2. Build a box from reclaimed pallet wood to fit the dimensions of your windows.
3. Make the back slightly higher than the front and cut the sides on a slant to tilt the windows forward and let in maximum light.
4. Attach the windows to the top edge with hinges and add wooden props to hold them open. Your cold frame is ready to use!

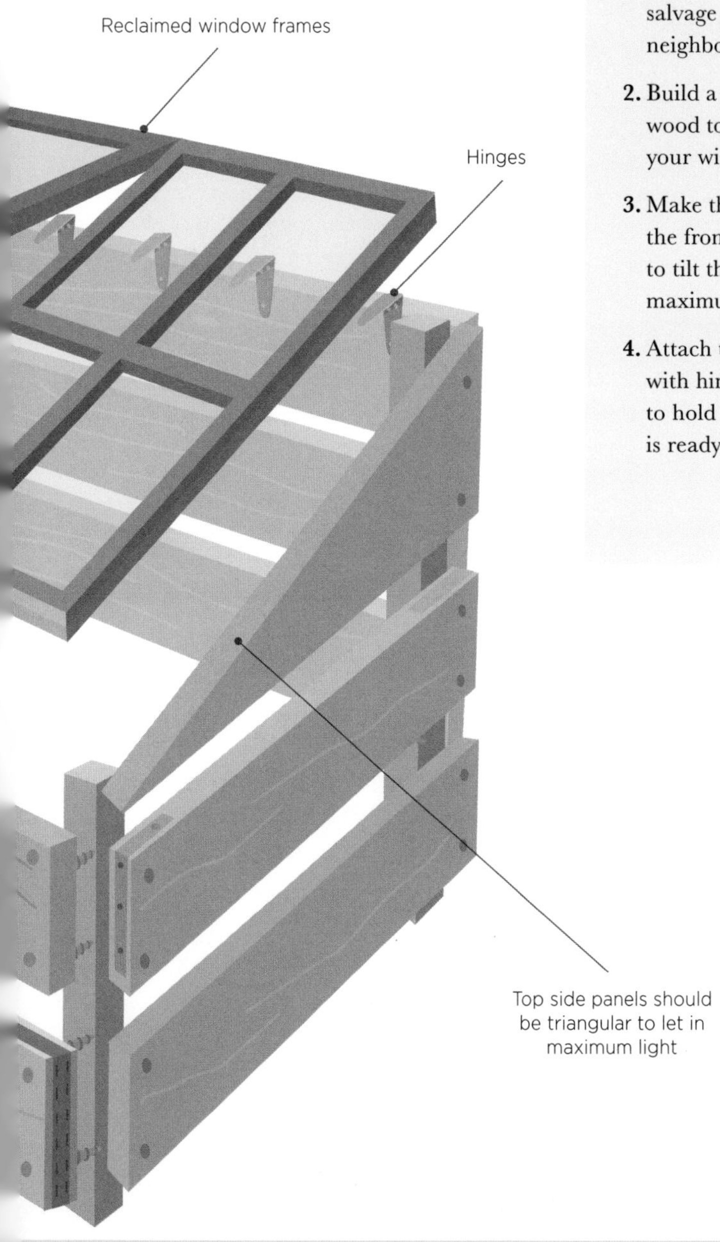

How to make compost

Making your own compost is the ultimate in recycling. Take day-to-day waste from your kitchen and garden, add water, come back a while later and ta-da! Your rubbish is now dark, rich, sweet-smelling compost.

Compost is soil food – it turbocharges growth by boosting the soil's ecosystem, plugging your plants into a web of fungi, bacteria and nematodes working unseen beneath your feet to help roots access water and nutrients.

You'll want to add it to your vegetable beds by the barrowload (about one barrow per square metre for mulching). So use several compost bins – three bins side by side, each at least $1m^2$ ($3ft^2$), gives you one to fill, one to rot and one full of finished compost ready to use.

Aim for a 50:50 mix of fast-rotting 'greens' – kitchen waste, grass clippings and plant material – and slower-rotting 'browns' such as straw, paper and shredded prunings. Mix up your ingredients every few months by turning it – fork everything out of the bin, then back in again (if your bins are in a row, just fork everything from one bin into the next). You should have finished compost in about a year; it's ready once it's dark brown, even textured and you can't see individual ingredients.

Make your own bins

Make bins from second-hand boards or pallet wood, leaving narrow gaps between the boards to allow air in. Nail pairs of 5 x 5cm (2 x 2in) uprights to each side at the front edge to make slots and slide boards in as you fill your bin, removing them to empty it again.

Small space composting

No room for compost bins? You can still make compost!

- **Wormeries** take up no more room than a dustbin. The volume of compost is small, but you do get to drain off worm wee to make five-star liquid plant food.
- **Bokashi bins** fit onto a kitchen worktop; layer food (cooked and uncooked) with specially inoculated Bokashi bran and it ferments into bacteria-rich pre-compost to add to soil.
- **In-ground composting** can be achieved by digging trenches and layering kitchen scraps and plant waste with newspaper creating enriched areas for planting hungry plants such as beans and courgettes.

TIP

Pallets make great compost bins; stand four on their edges to make a box and screw short boards across the corners to bolt them together. To empty, simply take the whole thing apart again.

DIY potting composts

Garden compost is also an essential ingredient in homemade potting composts – by far the greenest kind as they're peat-free, there's no plastic sack and the ingredients come from your back garden, so they have the very lowest of carbon footprints.

Making compost

Every gardener has their own recipes, and homemade potting mixes are infinitely tweakable; add sand or grit for extra drainage, lime for brassicas or composted bracken for acid-loving plants such as blueberries.

But for most plants, a basic recipe is all you need. Use a spade to measure out ingredients if you're making a barrowload, or a trowel for smaller quantities.

Seed compost for sowing seeds

- One part garden soil
- One part leaf mould or well-rotted (two years or more) woodchip
- Sieve with a fine riddle before using

Standard multipurpose mix for potting on and annual containers

- Two parts garden soil
- One part leaf mould or well-rotted woodchip
- Three parts homemade garden compost
- One part sand or grit for drainage
- One trowel full of seaweed meal fertilizer per barrowload
- Mix thoroughly and sieve through an 8mm (¼in) mesh

GO GREENER

Perlite, vermiculite and hydroleca are often used to improve drainage in potting mixes - but all have sky-high carbon footprints. Lower-carbon alternatives include crushed seashells and horticultural grit.

Long-term compost for potted fruit trees and herbs

- Two parts garden soil
- One part leaf mould or well-rotted woodchip
- Two parts homemade garden compost
- One part sand or grit
- One trowel full of seaweed meal fertilizer per barrowload
- Adding garden compost keeps soil light and open – this is essential in containers

Making leaf mould

Fallen autumn leaves are treasure to green gardeners, as they're the raw material for leaf mould – a wonderful low-nutrient, water-retentive ingredient for homemade potting mixes. Collect leaves from deciduous trees – oak, beech or hornbeam make the best leaf mould – and stack separately from your other compost. Knock four posts into the ground and wrap chicken wire round them to make a bin, then heap in your leaves. Or fill dumpy bags or old compost sacks instead, punching a few holes for drainage. Allow to rot for two years for potting-grade leaf mould, which makes a fantastic mulch.

Should I sterilize compost?

Sterilizing seed compost by baking it in the oven for 20 minutes at 85°C (185°F), or for a lower-energy option, zapping it in the microwave (90 seconds per kilo; 2.2 lbs of dampened soil in a plastic container) kills weed seeds and diseases – but it's high-energy, fairly impractical and destroys beneficial soil organisms, too. So, though it's a little riskier, it's usually better to leave seed compost unsterilized and nip out weed seedlings as they appear.

Buying compost sustainably

Not everyone can make their own potting mix, so sometimes buying it in bags is the only option. But rather than grabbing the first sack you see, take a moment to find out what's in the bag and where it's come from.

Until recently, peat has been the main ingredient in nearly all blends. But extracting peat for use in potting composts actively contributes to climate change, releasing thousands of years' worth of sequestered carbon into the air as the greenhouse gas carbon dioxide. It also destroys a unique biosphere, along with rare and unusual plants and animals found nowhere else. In fact, using peat to grow plants is right up there with plastic and pesticides in the environmental damage stakes.

There are now dozens of brands of good peat-free compost. Ask friends for recommendations or check out peat-free comparison trials carried out by professional gardeners and research organizations. Stick to the leading brands and you won't go far wrong.

Other ingredients have an environmental impact, too. Coir is transported from South Asia and needs lots of water for processing in an area of the world where water is at a premium; synthetic fertilizers carry a sky-high carbon footprint. And if the bark in your compost is shipped from Spain, your compost gets less green by the spadeful.

So, make sure your potting composts are peat-free, certified organic and made from ingredients grown close to where the compost is made. It takes a little detective work to find them, but they're well worth tracking down.

ECO WORRIER

Some of the world's peat bogs are so damaged, they have switched from the best carbon stores to net emitters of greenhouse gases, giving off millions of tonnes of CO_2 a year – though the picture is gradually improving as peat restoration projects gather pace.

Buy compost without the plastic

Every 50L of compost you buy comes with a side order of plastic sack, so go for these alternatives:

Bags for life Peat-free manufacturer Melcourt is pioneering refillable compost sacks; if your garden centre doesn't stock them, ask why not.

↑ **Loose loads** If you have room, the same local company will usually deliver compost loose to your door in a plastic-free heap.

→ **Bulk buying** Get compost delivered from a local company in 1t (1.10tn) bulk bags and share with friends, or buy from an allotment trading hut.

Gardening without peat

The best peat-free composts have held their own against peat-based in comparison trials for years – sometimes outperforming them completely. But their higher levels of organic materials mean you may have to tweak your usual gardening routine to help them perform at their best.

Watering

The organic matter in peat-free compost holds on to water like a sponge, so you'll sometimes find peat-free composts need watering less often – though it does vary between brands.

But with peat-free composts, it's sometimes hard to tell whether plants need watering, as the surface can look dry even when there's a soggy bottom beneath! So, before you water, stick your finger into the compost – if your fingertip feels dry, water away.

On the plus side, peat-free compost is easier to re-wet than peat-based compost – so if you forget to water, it's easier to put things right again.

ECO WORRIER

Though peat bogs cover just 3% of the Earth's surface, they sequester more carbon than all the world's forests combined.

Feeding

Getting the nutrients right can be the biggest challenge in switching to peat-free. All that organic matter also contains lots of active microbes – great for your plants, but also prone to hogging nitrogen, leaving little left for seedlings.

Start adding a weekly dose of liquid feed to the water almost straight away – certainly within a couple of weeks of seedlings emerging or potting up plants. Organic liquid seaweed or homemade nettle tea (see page 68) are ideal for young plants.

Add extra slow-release fertilizer such as seaweed meal to boost your peat-free compost, or cut in some garden soil – one part soil to three parts peat-free compost adds bulk and nutrients to the mix.

Watering tip

It helps if you stand pots in a tray while you're watering to catch any run-off and prevent precious nutrients leaching out. Watering little and often keeps peat-free composts moist without washing out all the goodness. Pots do not like to stand in water for long periods of time, so be careful not to overwater.

Storing your compost

How you keep your compost really matters. The nutrients in peat-free compost wash out easily, and wet compost that's stored for too long can turn stagnant – and is lethal to plants.

So, avoid buying compost that's been sitting in the garden centre over winter, especially if it's kept outside. And once you get it home, pop it in a secure container in a sheltered spot, perhaps in the shed or in a cool, dark place where it's out of the rain, and use it within six months, so it's nice and fresh.

No-dig gardening

There's a whole world under your feet. Healthy garden soil is teeming with microorganisms, all interconnected in a web of relationships – many of which help your plants plug into water and nutrients more easily. So, take good care of your soil, and your garden grows better.

As discussed on page 30, digging breaks up that fragile ecosystem, fracturing the delicate chains of beneficial bacteria and mycorrhizal fungi linking your plants' roots into the earth. Leave your spade in the shed and the underground biome thrives undisturbed, allowing new, more complex connections to form.

Spread organic mulches across the soil and you feed all that subterranean life, boosting it even further. As microorganism populations boom, plants find it easier to access the minerals they need, and your soil becomes better aerated. At the same time, more humus is pulled down into the soil, turning it dark, crumbly and rich. It's a gradual process, so it may be a few years before you notice a difference – but keep it up and the soil gets better and better.

Mulches

As well as feeding your soil's ecosystem – and therefore your plants – organic mulches lock in moisture, so they help drought-proof your garden in hot summers. No-dig methods also make it easier to garden on claggy clay soils. Instead of the back-breaking labour of turning heavy, sticky clods, simply leave the soil undisturbed, cover it with mulch and plant or sow into that – no spade, or sore back, required.

Use well-rotted mulches where you're planting or sowing, or lay fresh greenery on the ground around established plants to break down naturally over time.

Here are six of the best organic no-dig mulches:

Garden compost Recycled garden waste is free and sustainable, but it's hard to make enough.

Farmyard or stable manure Make sure that the manure is well-rotted; if not, add it to your compost heap first.

Municipal green waste Buy from your local recycling depot – it's sterilized to kill weeds and diseases.

Woodchip Use small amounts of shredded or chipped felled trees and branches.

Grass clippings Lay on the soil around plants, pulled back from stems.

Comfrey leaves A source of potassium for flowering crops such as courgettes and peas.

Looking after a no-dig garden

Managing no-dig gardens is mostly about keeping the soil covered at all times – you should be looking at mulch or lush, leafy plants in a no-dig vegetable garden, never bare earth.

Top up mulches once a year – usually in autumn as you clear spent plants from vegetable beds, though you can mulch any time if you need to. Always mulch onto damp earth (water first if conditions are dry) and spread in a thin layer, about 5cm (2in) deep.

It's hard to make all the mulch you need yourself. A standard metre-square compost bin makes enough compost to mulch 10–15m^2 (107–161ft^2); if you're gardening an allotment, at 250m^2 (2,690ft^2), that's a lot of compost bins. So, most no-dig gardeners top up from outside sources.

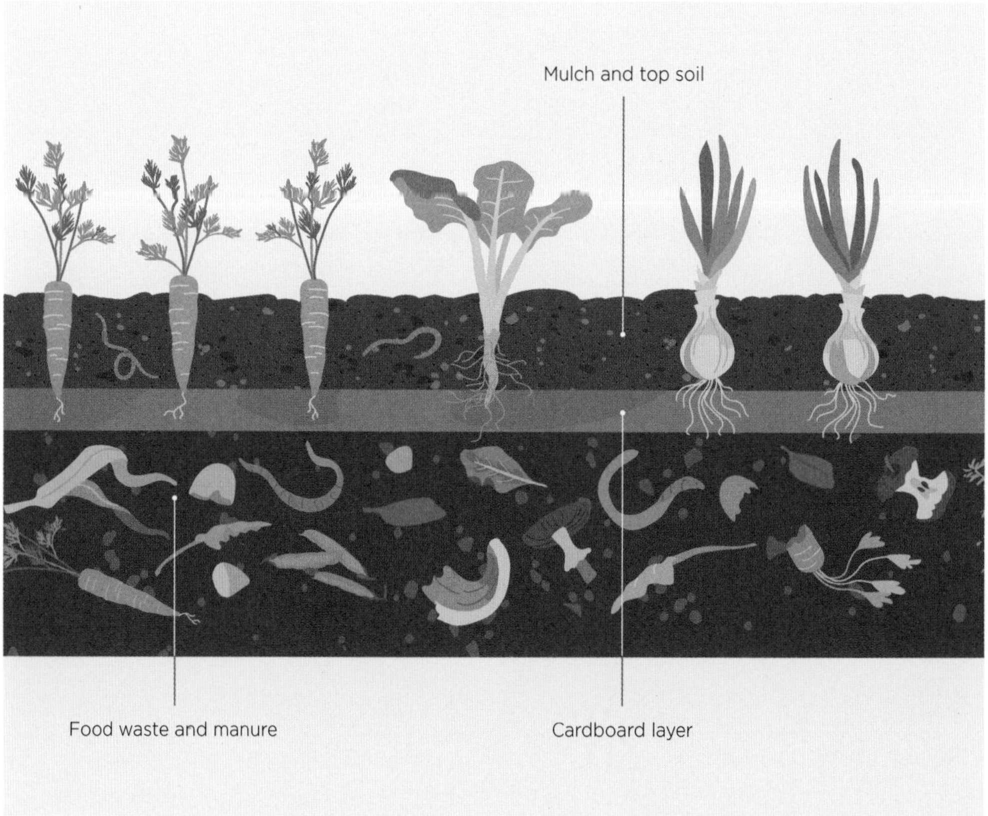

No-dig green manures

Green manures can be a really useful backup to the annual autumn mulch, growing quickly into a thick green carpet that smothers weeds and helps the soil hold on to nutrients.

Conventional winter manures such as grazing rye are traditionally dug into the soil in spring. An easier option (especially in no-dig systems) is to grow annual green manures such as phacelia, buckwheat and mustard. These die back in cold weather, leaving a dense thatch of dead top growth on the surface of the soil, just like a mulch. Simply rake off in spring before replanting and add to the compost heap.

Ask local stables if they'll let you raid the muck heap, or find out if any nearby farms have biodigesters and will let you take some of the organic digestate that's left as a by-product. You can also buy municipal green waste by the tonne – but it's expensive and delivery carries a relatively high carbon cost. Alternatively, make up the shortfall with green manures, covering the ground with dense, nutritious greenery instead.

You can sow and plant directly into fully rotted organic mulches. Weeding in a no-dig system is usually easier, as mulches bury most annual weed seeds out of trouble. But perennial weeds will still come through, and some annuals will blow in, too, so hoe once a week, working the blade across the mulch to slice off top growth just below the surface. For more on dealing with weeds, see page 86.

GO GREENER

More than 80% of the carbon in your garden is held in the soil, but digging releases it as the greenhouse gas carbon dioxide. Leave your soil undisturbed and you also keep the carbon it contains safely locked away.

Feeding your plants

Just like people, plants need a good all-round range of nutrients to grow and thrive. But simply plying your plants with lots of artificial fertilizer isn't the answer. In fact, a fast-food diet is just as bad for vegetables as it is for us, leading to sappy, weak, disease-prone plants. Focus instead on feeding your soil.

Artificial fertilizer also has a sky-high carbon footprint. It requires lots of energy to manufacture and its use (particularly if it has a high nitrogen component) will release the greenhouse gas nitrous oxide – actively contributing to climate change. Use organic alternatives such as hoof and horn, dried blood and lucerne pellets.

A healthy garden soil already holds all the nutrients your plants need, so you shouldn't need extra fertilizers at all. Concentrate on the quality of your soil, restoring its natural balance with annual mulches of organic matter (see page 63) to return humus removed through harvesting, weeding and pruning, and your plants should thrive.

The only time you may need to add extra fertilizer is when you're starting a new vegetable plot on soil that hasn't been cultivated for a while. Just for the first couple of seasons, while organic matter is building in your soil, help crops along with slow-release organic fertilizers, such as the aforementioned and seaweed meal scattered in spring.

GO GREENER

Grow beans and peas. They'll trap nitrogen from the air, and when you compost the bits you don't need they will eventually deliver the nitrogen back to the soil.

Chlorosis (leaf yellowing) in chalky soil

Club root in brassicas

Blossom end rot in tomatoes

Mineral deficiencies

Soils with chronic shortages of minerals are, thankfully, rare, though it's worth testing your soil just in case (the RHS offers a comprehensive soil-testing service for members). But sometimes minerals become less available to your plants, and you may need to change the way you garden to keep your plants healthy.

	Alkaline/chalky soil	Acid soil	Dry soil
Problem	Iron and manganese can become locked up	Brassicas struggle to access molybdenum	Tomatoes can't absorb calcium
Appearance	Young leaves appear yellow on acid-loving plants such as raspberries and blueberries	Stunted whiptail growth of brassicas. Clubroot thrives in acidic soils.	Blossom end rot in tomatoes Apples develop a bitter pit
Solution	Mulch with compost or shredded bracken Grow blueberries in containers of ericaceous (acidic) compost instead	Add wood ash or sustainably harvested oragnic calcified seaweed. The latter needs to be added to the soil at least three months before planting	Aim for even levels of soil moisture at all times - mulches will help (for more on watering, see page 74)

Good diets for potted vegetable plots

When you grow plants in containers and greenhouses, they can't plug into soil nutrients in the same way as those in the ground, so as well as watering, it's up to you to provide their dietary needs with regular doses of fertilizer.

Potting compost contains some fertilizer and will provide for their needs for a short time, but you can't rely on it for long. So, plan a feeding regime for all your container- and greenhouse-grown plants to start within a couple of weeks of potting up.

Feed once a week from spring until late summer while plants are in active growth – it helps to get into a routine and do it on the same day every week, so you don't forget. Never feed onto dry compost; if necessary, water once, then come back after an hour and water again with liquid feed added.

B **Liquid seaweed** is a good all-round, general-purpose tonic you can use on just about anything – it's also one of the most sustainably sourced of all organic fertilizers.

C **Nitrogen-rich nettle or compost tea** (see overleaf) is ideal for promoting the growth and health of seedlings. Although fairly weak, these homemade fertilizers can be used with the season-long feeding of leafy spinach, salads and brassicas. When fruiting vegetable plants (such as tomatoes and courgettes) start to flower, switch to comfrey fertilizer instead, as this has a potassium component that prompts flowers to convert to fruit.

FEEDING SCHEDULE

DO

- Start feeding overwintered tender herbs and potted fruit with liquid seaweed at the first signs of new growth in spring.
- Continue feeding leafy vegetables in containers throughout summer with nettle, compost or seaweed feed. Switch to comfrey tea for flowering crops such as tomatoes, courgettes and fruit.
- Stop feeding as growth slows in autumn; this also helps tomatoes concentrate on ripening the last green fruits.

DON'T

- Overfeed young vegetables. Dilute liquid seaweed feed to half strength for the youngest seedlings, then bump up to full strength once you start potting them into individual containers.
- Feed vegetables in early autumn or winter, as any tender new growth promoted by the fertilizer can be damaged by cold weather.
- Feed plants in the dormant season - autumn and winter - as any nutrients will be wasted.

Making your own fertilizers

Homemade feed comes plastic-free, with a near-zero carbon footprint – and you grow it yourself! You can turn most plant material into homemade liquid fertilizer simply by allowing it to rot and release the nutrients it holds, making a concentrated liquid you can then dilute and water on. Soaking compost and manure is even quicker, yielding 'tea' within just a few days.

Most plant material contains varying levels of nitrogen (for leafy growth), phosphorus (for roots) and potassium (for flowers and fruit) – the three main nutrients needed for growth. But some major on one particular nutrient, allowing you to make targeted feeds.

Comfrey leaves, for example, contain as much nitrogen and phosphorus as farmyard manure, but three times as much potassium, making the leaves a suitable choice for feeding flowering greenhouse plants such as tomatoes and cucumbers.

There's little research into the most effective way of making and using homemade fertilizers, so it's an inexact science. Most will be quite weak – some more than others, depending on how they are made. As a rule of thumb, start by adding a mugful of concentrate to a 5L (10pt) watering can and see what colour it comes out; adjust until it's the colour of weak tea, and it's ready to water onto your plants.

TIP

Next time you're pulling perennial weeds, get your own back by dunking them, roots and all, in water for a month to convert them into a liquid food for your plants.

Five homemade fertilizers

Compost tea Suspend a hessian bag of compost or well-rotted manure in a little water, add 5tbsp of sugar and an aquarium pump to turbocharge beneficial bacteria within two days.

Comfrey tea Plant the variety Bocking 14, which doesn't self-seed, and harvest up to three times a year, slicing young leaves away just above ground level.

Nettle tea Don some gauntlets before cutting nettles while they're young – no more than 25–30cm (10–12in) tall and still bright green – to benefit from the higher nitrogen levels.

Seaweed Ask the harbourmaster for permission to collect seaweed from the high tide line. Rinse in fresh water to dilute the saltiness before chopping up and spreading on the soil.

Worm wee Collect the dark brown liquid dripping from your wormery to make a lovely rich liquid plant food; dilute as for other liquid feeds before using.

Comfrey plants are also great for pollinators.

Two ways to make liquid fertilizer

Make batches of fertilizer to bottle and use on containers and greenhouse crops. Homemade fertilizers extract the goodness from nutrient-rich greenery and turn them into rich liquid feeds to boost your plants. You can do it two ways: with water (smelly, but easy) or without, for a more concentrated brew.

Method 1: Sink 'n' soak

This is quick and easy – but smells really bad once it's nearly ready, so make it well away from the house.

1. Harvest leafy material while it's still young and green, or collect together a good pile of grass clippings, seaweed or weeds.
2. Pack them into a 15L (26pt) bucket, cramming them in tightly – the more you get in, the richer your feed.
3. Now put a brick on top to hold everything in place and and half-fill the bucket with water.
4. Seal the bucket with a board or a lid – this keeps rainwater out, and the smell in!
5. Set this aside for three to four weeks, checking and mixing occasionally. Once the leaves are fully rotted, decant off the liquid into a bottle.

Break up leaves if necessary to get more into your bucket

Method 2: Drainpipe 'n' drip

This is the non-smelly method – it takes a little longer to get going, but then provides a steady supply throughout the season.

1. Fix a 1m (3ft) length of wide drainpipe to a shed wall or fencepost.
2. Staple fine-gauge wire mesh across the bottom end to prevent blockages, before fitting a funnel to direct the liquid into a bucket below.
3. Chop up leaves, then pack them tightly into the pipe until it's about two-thirds full.
4. Fill a 1L (2pt) drinks bottle with sand and tie string to the neck. Thread a disc of wood onto the string, a little wider than the pipe to make a rainproof lid.
5. Lower the bottle into the pipe until it rests on the chopped leaves and place the lid on the pipe. In a few weeks, dark brown liquid should start dripping from the funnel for you to bottle. Keep your comfrey tea coming by adding more chopped leaves to the top of the drainpipe as the level drops.

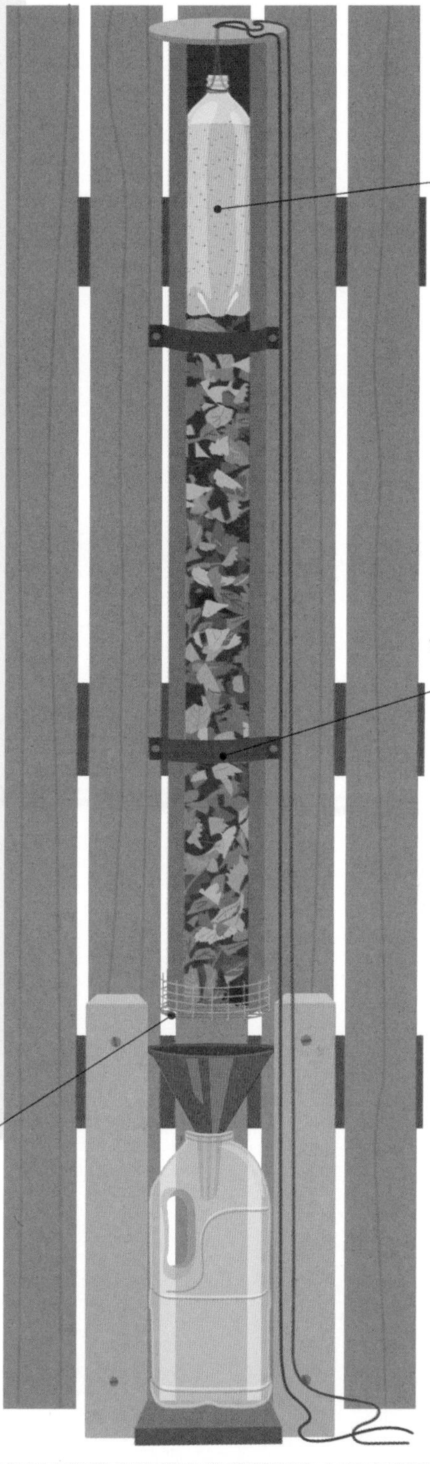

Watering your vegetable garden

In today's climate-changed world, how we water our gardens has never mattered more. Water is a precious resource to be used thoughtfully – and only when absolutely necessary. Yet, every summer brings new record-breaking heatwaves, and our gardens depend on us for water more than they've ever needed to before.

Vegetables in particular need careful watering as your harvest depends on it. As a rule of thumb, in the open garden start watering only once there has been no proper rain for a fortnight (short, light showers don't count). Then, water thoroughly, drenching the soil right down to the rootzone (test with a spade after an hour – the soil should be damp to the blade's end).

Water in the morning or evening (to minimize evaporation) and use a second-hand galvanized, plastic-free watering can – this lets you direct water precisely where it's needed.

Target supplies on vegetables that need it most. Good practice is to water the soil the day before sowing, then leave until the seedlings emerge before watering again. In summer, sow seeds slightly deeper. Water seedlings twice weekly for the first few weeks after they emerge, plus young vegetables recently transplanted outside, and thirsty vegetables (see box opposite).

Every 10 days or so, soak leafy vegetables and any plants in flower (peas, beans, courgettes and the like). In prolonged droughts, give the whole garden a deep soak once a fortnight. Water big plots in rotation, dividing it into sections to save effort. Increased spacing between plants also means that each plant has more soil to explore for water: 30 per cent opening out can be significant.

Drought-proof your vegetable patch

There's lots you can do to buffer your vegetable plot against the vagaries of our climate-changed weather.

Mulch, mulch, mulch A layer of organic matter (see page 63) locks in moisture and boosts organic matter in the soil, helping it hold more water.

Plant in channels This will help give the water a chance to soak into the rootzone instead of running off.

Group plants together Rather then trying to fit it all in one pot, group several for combined shelter and shade.

Keep weeds down Weeds hog available moisture, so keep areas near crops free of competition. Thick mulches will also help stop weed growth.

Water into clay pots Sink clay pots next to thirsty crops and fill with water to seep gradually into the soil.

Use self-watering pots These pots have a built-in reservoir, so plants can draw up what they need straight into the rootzone.

Thirsty...

Thirsty vegetables
Clockwise from top left: runner beans, lettuce, Florence fennel, celery and spinach

...not thirsty

Drought-tolerant vegetables
Clockwise from top left: chard, beetroot, turnips, carrots and parsnips

Harvesting the rain

The best drink you can give to your plants simply falls from the sky. Rain requires no treatment with chemicals, you don't have to transport it to your home and plants prefer it, as it contains tiny amounts of growth-boosting nitrogen.

Storing water

The main difficulty for gardeners is that you either have far too much rain – or not quite enough. When rain is plentiful to the point of overstaying its welcome, it's usually winter, plants are dormant and there's no need to water. Then, in summer, when your plants are at their thirstiest, the rain clouds vanish and there's not a drop to be had for week after endlessly sunny week.

The answer to this conundrum is to save as much rain in times of plenty to store ready for periods of drought.

The exact amount of rainwater you'll need to save depends on your local climate, the type of soil you have and what you grow. But if space isn't an issue, aim for enough storage to hold about 1,000L (264gal) of rainwater for an allotment-sized 250m^2 (2,690ft^2) vegetable plot, then add more if necessary.

That sounds like a lot, but it's only five large water butts; connect two butts together to add to downpipes from your shed and house roofs, plus one on the greenhouse, and you're sorted. You can even bury rainwater-harvesting tanks underground where they're all but invisible. If they're large enough, you can harvest enough rainwater to supply your house, too.

GO GREENER

Repurposed second-hand galvanized steel water tanks and cattle troughs make great plastic-free water butts. Add a wooden lid and simply dip your watering can in the top.

Water storage in small spaces

If space is short, you can still save a surprising amount. Slimline water butts fit flush to the wall, taking up hardly any room. And even balconies can squeeze in a rain saucer – a framework like an upside-down umbrella, lined with waterproof membrane to catch and funnel rain into freestanding containers beneath.

Build a freestanding rain harvester

Make a simple wooden structure to catch rain without a building nearby.

1. Get hold of two or three identical tanks or water butts and stand them side by side on reclaimed bricks, so you can get a watering can underneath the taps.
2. Build an open frame around them from reclaimed pallet wood or decking, with the front edge just above the water butts, and the back edge slightly higher.
3. Nail planks across the top of the structure to make a sloping roof, and place a corrugated sheet on top of them.
4. Attach guttering to the lower edge of the roof, with a downpipe feeding into one of the water butts – and wait for a rainy day!

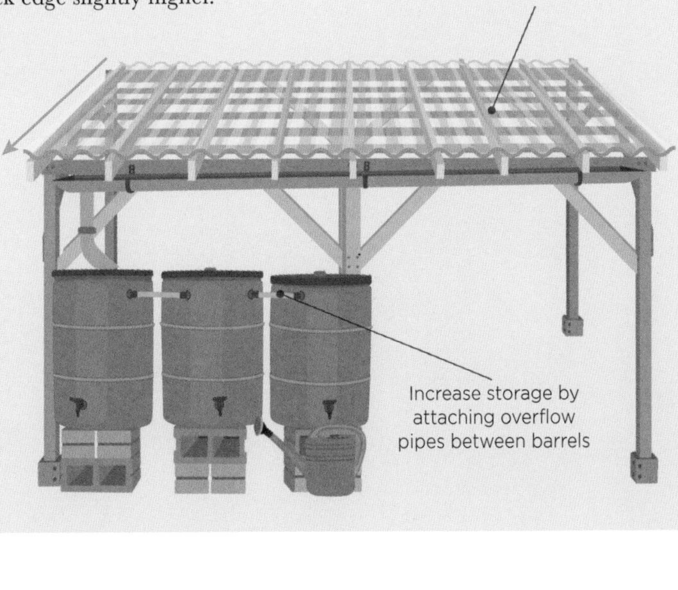

Unexpected visitors

We gardeners are, it's fair to say, conflicted about the wildlife we share our gardens with. We bend over backwards to create havens for birds, bees, butterflies and hedgehogs – but show us a slug, aphid or vine weevil and the red mist descends.

Perhaps a change of heart is needed. After all, slugs, aphids and vine weevils play just as important a part in your garden's wider ecosystem as butterflies and bees. They may be annoyingly fond of eating your crops, but they also do valuable jobs, such as breaking down dead plant material. They're also an important food source for other creatures – get rid of them and you drive away the birds, ladybirds and hedgehogs that feed on them, too.

Instead, think in terms of protecting your plants – you'll keep plants safest when you stop them coming to harm in the first place, using barriers or disease-resistant varieties. Next best is to keep the number of troublesome bugs at manageable levels – keep a close eye on your crops and at the first inkling of an infestation, take action.

Only if you're losing the battle do you need the big guns. Organic, plant-based pesticides (such as those based on rape-seed oil or soapy, fatty acids) can help get infestations back under control, but there is a chance they'll kill beneficial insects as well as the unwanted ones. A well-managed garden is a form of prevention in itself, suffering fewer infestations than those that are less cared for.

GO GREENER

Try biodegradable insect mesh, made from corn starch, stretched over sturdy wooden frames to make a plastic-free alternative for keeping caterpillars off brassicas.

It's a lucky gardener that has a regular song thrush visitor, these birds love to eat snails.

Six sustainable ways to protect your crops

Garden hygiene
Keep working areas tidy so bugs can't overwinter, and disinfect pruning secateurs against disease.

Barriers
Cages of insect-proof netting held away from the foliage also protects from birds; mesh fencing buried up to 60cm (24in) deep, keeps rabbits out.

Physical removal
Wipe aphids off shoot tips or with a jet of water. Inspect seedling trays daily for lurking slugs and pick off diseased foliage.

Deterrents
Standing containers on pot feet in saucers of water deters slugs; spraying with chilli or garlic soaked water may put off any sap-sucking insects.

Disease-resistant varieties
Look for varieties with genetic resistance to disease, such as blight-resistant potatoes and clubroot-tolerant brassicas.

Biological controls
Harness natural predators by releasing predatory wasps against whitefly, and watering on nematodes against pests like leatherjackets, vine weevil and slugs.

Crop rotation the sustainable way

You'll go a long way towards helping your crops fend off unwanted insects and diseases simply by moving them around the plot each year so they're never growing in the same place for too long.

Traditional crop rotation works on the idea that vegetables come in 'families' affected by the same problems. Cabbage root fly, for example, attacks all kinds of brassicas from kale to cabbages, but doesn't affect peas (or other legumes). Grow closely related vegetables together and move them onto fresh soil each season, and insects and diseases have to start from scratch.

This idea has its limits, though. Crop rotation won't trouble carrot fly, nor will it stop your potatoes getting blight, which drifts for miles. In small gardens it's hard to move your crops far enough to make a difference, but if you have the space, crop rotation is good practice and goes hand in hand with looking after your soil.

Growing crops in the same family together makes them easier to look after, as they often need the same care.

Mix it up

Don't get too hung up on rotating your crops – as long as you don't grow exactly the same crop in exactly the same place year after year, you won't go far wrong. It can be as effective to mix up your crops instead. Insects find it harder to identify target plants when they're jumbled up with distracting flowers and herbs; mixed plants use a broader cross-section of nutrients, too, so your soil stays more balanced.

In fact, there's evidence that some plants grow better in groups, and you can use this in your garden, too. Grow your crops in planned 'guilds' and every plant brings something to the party. Legumes pull nitrogen into the soil; broad squash leaves reduce moisture loss and keep out weeds. Others deter unwanted critters, pull minerals from the subsoil or draw in pollinating insects. Start with permanently planted fruit, shrubby herbs and perennial crops (see page 116), then add annual crops to the mix.

Planting nasturtiums alongside beans is an excellent way to decoy blackfly away from your crop.

Build your guild

Group these crops together, or some of these crops together in the same bed and everything benefits. The inclusion of fruit like apples and blackcurrants expands the range:

Apple trees Blossom for pollinators; sequesters carbon

Blackcurrants Shelters other vegetables

Onions (perennial) Said to deter root fly on carrots, parsnips, parsley, celery and celeriac

Carrots Deep roots mine minerals

Kale Allow to flower for pollinators

Climbing beans (French and runner) Allow for vertical planting

Oregano Attracts pollinators

Nasturtium Living mulch; pollinator attracting; decoys blackfly away from beans

Clover Nitrogen fixing; living mulch

Legumes (peas, beans, etc.) Nitrogen fixing

Tackling insect outbreaks

Sometimes, however vigilant you are, unwanted visitors get through even your best defences and start causing serious damage to your crops, leaving you with little choice but to fight back. Reaching for the spray gun is always a last resort, to be used only in emergencies.

Using sprays as a last resort

Insecticidal sprays, even if they're organic, kill indiscriminately, so if you spray aphids, you'll also kill any ladybirds in the area, too. And, since aphids breed so fast – they can triple their populations within a week – they'll be back a lot sooner than the ladybirds.

Oil-based sprays are made from plant oils such as sunflower and rapeseed, and work by blocking spiracles (breathing holes). They are less likely to harm larger nontarget bugs such as bees and ladybirds – though they will kill smaller beneficial insects. They're usually a kinder choice than broad-spectrum pyrethrum pesticides (made from plant extracts), which, although organic, can kill almost everything they come into contact with.

Use organic sprays only when outbreaks are starting to cause real harm and you have exhausted all other options. Even then, use only a minimal amount, following the manufacturer's instructions carefully. Spray in the early morning or evening when bees are less likely to be around. And as soon as you have the problem under control, stop.

GO GREENER

Gardens managed without pesticides are almost certainly going to be richer in insects, which feed birds and foster their populations.

Greener options

There are also a few other, more sustainable, methods to try:

➲ **Spray with water** Turn your hose to a high-pressure jet setting and blast shoot tips and foliage to control outbreaks of blackfly on beans or woolly aphid on kale. Turn the hose to a fine spray and mist crops that are suffering from red spider mite to increase humidity.

➲ **Grow carnivorous plants** Pop a potted sundew (*Drosera*) in the greenhouse and it will happily devour whitefly and fungus gnats all summer. Pitcher plants (*Sarracenia*) or Venus flytraps will catch larger flies. Grow in specialist peat-free ericaceous compost and keep well-watered with rainwater.

➲ **Plant biofumigants** Some plants send out underground self-defence chemicals capable of suppressing soil annoyances such as wireworms and potato cyst nematodes. Grow 'Caliente' mustard or rocket as a summer green manure, then finely chop foliage and mix it into the soil. Water the surface and cover with an impermeable sheet to trap the biofumigant gases, then uncover the ground two weeks before sowing or planting.

The scattergun approach

Sustainable gardening is all about seeing your garden as a whole: a big, beautiful, complicated ecosystem kept perfectly in balance just the way nature designed it, allowing your plants to thrive.

It's the same when it comes to keeping your plants safe. Instead of relying on just one defence strategy, deploy multiple tactics at once to head off would-be problems from all directions.

This scattergun approach to plant protection, known as integrated pest management, builds a phalanx of protective strategies into your growing routine from seed to harvest. It creates a protective shield around your plants keeping them safe from almost all the troubles that might beset them – without ever having to rely on chemicals.

This doesn't mean eliminating all problems altogether: the aim is to keep them to a manageable level. So you still get a few aphids, some slugs and a smattering of spotty leaves, but they never get to a level where they seriously affect the growth of your plants.

TIP

Prevent mildew on courgettes by spraying with a plant invigorator such as SB Plant Invigorator, which works by boosting the plants' health and resistance to some pests and diseases.

A five-step strategy to keep your plants safe

Use these methods simultaneously and you'll head off most problems before they get serious.

1. Garden well The better your grow your plants, the easier they'll shrug off disease and grow through a little insect damage – so make sure your plants have all the sunshine, good soil and attention that they need.

➋ 2. Stay vigilant Inspect plants daily to spot problems before they get serious, paying close attention to vulnerable areas like shoot tips. Pheromone traps also give you early warning when insects like codling moths and pea moths are on the wing.

3. Keep it clean Remove yellowing and diseased leaves promptly, and quarantine new plants for a month before you put them in the garden until you're sure they're not carrying unwanted hitchhikers.

4. Prevent problems where possible Build barriers and fencing from the start to keep pigeons and insects at bay, encourage a diverse ecosystem full of natural predators and grow resistant varieties to reduce disease.

➊ 5. Act early When you do get an outbreak, limit the damage by removing affected foliage promptly to limit the spread of disease, or targeting specific problems with biological controls such as nemotodes (see page 79).

When is a weed not a weed?

Many of the plants that gardeners refer to as 'weeds' are really just wildflowers with a PR problem. Some are downright beneficial, helping to improve soil, attract pollinators and even draw up minerals to help feed your plants.

Know when to pull

The problems start when these natural pioneers do what they do best: grow, fast. These are nature's colonizers, and the most troublesome spread so vigorously they swamp your crops, out-competing them for space, water and nutrients, and seriously affecting your harvest – sometimes bringing it to a halt altogether.

Your job as gardener is to act as referee. It's not always necessary to weed out absolutely every new arrival – some are relatively benign, and indeed worth inviting in for the advantages they can bring to your crops, attracting pollinators to help beans set pods or drawing in growth-boosting nitrogen. Other beneficial blow-ins can be tolerated with careful managing: nipping off flowers as they go over and before they set seed, for example.

The ones to keep away from your vegetable beds are fast-spreading annuals such as cleavers, bittercress and groundsel, and thuggish perennial weeds, which will take over the whole space if you let them. Even then, if you can leave an unwanted corner of your vegetable garden away from your crops where they can grow undisturbed, they can still offer invaluable havens of food and habitat for wildlife.

To keep dandelions in check, it's best to remove the flowers before they have a chance to go to seed.

Helpful 'weeds'

Clover *Trifolium repens* Fixes nitrogen from the air, feeding the soil around it (not to be confused with yellow-flowered *Oxalis corniculata*, which looks similar but doesn't help your plants).

Herb robert *Geranium robertianum* Innocuous and pretty annual, which self-seeds readily but is easily controlled and rarely competes with crops; it brings in pollinating insects to boost your harvest.

Nettles *Urtica dioica* Best kept confined as it quickly swamps crops, but great for providing the raw materials for nettle feed and as a nursery for butterfly caterpillars.

Comfrey *Symphytum officinale* Draws up minerals from deep below ground, makes great plant food and bumblebees adore the flowers – though cut them back before they set seed.

Dandelions *Taraxacum officinale* Another mineral accumulator to help feed your crops, flowers are particularly rich in nectar – though remove them as they go over, before setting seed.

Keeping back invaders

Sometimes, you need to step in and evict uninvited gatecrashers before they hog all the food and drink and ruin the party. Unwanted weeds can get out of hand and swamp your crops within weeks if you let them take hold, so make it part of your weekly routine to keep them under strict control.

Hoe every week, before you even notice them growing, and you stop annual weeds long before they become a problem. Pull out any weeds growing close to existing crops with your fingers, or gently lever them out with a hand fork.

Digging out perennial weeds by the roots can sometimes feel like a fruitless task. Some roots grow up to 2m (7ft) deep into the soil, so you're unlikely to be able to remove them completely, especially as new shoots sprout from every broken underground root. Typical candidates are couch grass, ground elder and bindweed.

It is best, therefore, to dig out what you can and then concentrate on further weakening them by robbing them of the chance to photosynthesize. Chop off every new shoot that grows back just below ground level as part of your weekly hoeing routine, or pull them out with your fingers as soon as you see them. Keep this up for a few years and you will eventually get the upper hand with even the most persistent weeds.

Hoeing between plants each week keeps your vegetables free of competition.

Create a season of weed-free growing

This simple method holds back perennial weeds across a whole bed for the best part of a season, giving you months of blissfully weed-free growing.

1. In spring, remove all weedy top growth to ground level – no need to dig out any roots.
2. Cover the area with thick cardboard, overlapping the edges if necessary to ensure there are no gaps. Dampen, then tread down so it's snug against the soil.
3. Cover the whole area with a thick (10–15cm; 4–6in) mulch of homemade garden compost, municipal green waste or well-rotted farmyard manure.
4. Plant or sow into the mulch. Your plants root through the cardboard into the soil below, but the perennial weeds struggle to grow upwards. Once the cardboard breaks down and lets them through (usually after three to four months) revert to normal weeding or simply repeat the process. Allow to rot for two years for potting-grade leaf mould.

ECO WORRIER

The flowers and leaves of deep-rooted perennial dock support about 30 species of moth - some very rare - as well as the bats that feed on them. Fortunately docks are not rare!

Crops in pots

Not enough room in the garden – or no garden at all? No problem! It's amazing what you can grow in containers; in fact, your harvest from a well-planned patio vegetable plot can be as varied as any.

Modern breeding has produced 'patio' varieties of almost every kind of vegetable, bred to grow smaller than usual and with compact root systems, so they thrive in containers. They'll give you surprisingly generous harvests, too.

Choose a pint-sized version and you can even grow vegetable giants in pots: courgette 'Patio Star', runner bean 'Hestia' and pumpkin 'Jack Be Little' all grow happily in roomy (45–60cm; 18–24in) planters, but you may need to train the trailing shoots of the pumpkin up a support.

Easiest of all are fast-growing, shallow-rooted crops such as salads, herbs, spring onions, beetroot and leafy chard. You can also sow larger greens such as kale or pak choi thickly into containers to harvest at just 10cm (4in) tall as tender, tasty baby leaves.

Always plant into the largest containers you can find – it saves watering and gives vegetables more room to spread out.

Potted vegetable plots

Pack your pots with just one type of vegetable – or group crops together in potted vegetable plots. Choose combinations you use in your cooking and you can harvest your dinner in one go!

Roast dinner vegetable pot Pea 'Twinkle', round-rooted carrot 'Parmex' and beetroot 'Burpees Golden'. Plant the dwarf pea in the centre, with pea sticks for support, and resow the whole plot after harvesting.

Mediterranean cuisine Tomato 'Losetto', basil and French marigolds. This compact, blight-resistant cherry tomato grows in a natural bush shape; basil and marigolds help fend off unwelcome critters.

Healthy greens Calabrese 'Kabuki', kale 'Red Russian' and ruby chard. Plant the dwarf calabrese in the centre and sow kale and chard direct to pick young as nutritious summer greens.

Growing vegetables in containers

Your potted vegetables depend on you for all their needs, from water and food to light and shelter. So, look after container crops with care.

The larger your pots, the better, as big containers hold more water and give roots plenty of room. New clay pots carry a high carbon footprint, so second-hand pots are greener – and pre-aged, so they settle into your garden like they've always been there. Find them via online auctions or spend a happy afternoon hunting through local reclamation yards. You can also upcycle everything from bread bins to butler sinks into containers – or build your own planters from repurposed pallet wood.

Compost based on loam (soil) holds on to nutrients better than ordinary multipurpose potting mix – you can make your own (see page 54) or buy peat-free loam-based John Innes composts. Feed your crops weekly, adding liquid seaweed or nettle feed to the watering can while crops are young. When fruiting plants such as tomatoes and strawberries start to flower, switch to potassium-rich comfrey tea or organic tomato food (for leafy greens, stick with the nettle tea for its growth-boosting nitrogen).

Pre-aged pots are mixed with upcycled metal containers to create an eco-friendly and attractive corner in this garden.

A sunny, sheltered spot would suit more exotic plants such as these white chilli plants.

The amount of water your pots need can vary wildly – tomatoes get by on just 200ml (0.4pt) of water a day on dull days, but when it's sunny they'll get through 2L (4pt) each. Test whether pots need watering by lifting them up to see if they feel light or stick your finger into the compost to feel if it's damp beneath. You'll usually need to water at least once a day when the weather is dry – and sometimes on rainy days, too, as light rain just wets the surface without soaking in.

Pot-watering strategies

Group pots together in shade on sunny days.

Line clay pots with old compost bags to slow water loss.

Experiment with sheep's wool pellets by adding them to the compost as a way to retain moisture.

Stand pots in dishes or trays so that when you water there is a small pool of water at the base of the pot, which will be wicked up by the roots.

Make watering tubes from chicken wire filled with gravel and bury in the compost so that water is able to reach the centre of the compost, not just the top.

Holes in the base of the pot are essential so that plant roots do not accidentally become waterlogged.

GO GREENER

When resowing and replanting containers, there's no need to replace all the compost each time; just remove the top 5-10cm (2-4in) and replace with new.

Growing food without a garden

Growing your own vegetables isn't just for people with gardens. There are plenty of crops that thrive on balconies – and quite a few are happy with no more than a sunny windowsill.

TIP

Filter out stormy weather with reed screens attached to railings, and put up awnings to shade plants in extreme heat.

Windowsill allotments

Plant up your brightest, south- or west-facing windowsills with super-compact 'Twilight' chillies and micro cherry tomatoes, or plant a potted herb garden with parsley, Greek basil, mint and marjoram.

You can also fill trays with damp compost and sow thickly for microgreens (see page 112) – intensely flavoured seedling salads snipped at 5–7cm (2–3in) high. Peas, radish, red basil and sunflowers are particularly delicious.

Bounty on a balcony

Outdoor space is like gold dust when you live in an inner-city flat, so balconies are to be treasured. Clothe every inch in delicious things to pick and they can be surprisingly productive, too.

Plant a few larger containers rather than lots of little ones, as they hold on to water and feed better (lightweight wooden planters or upcycled tin baths put less weight on your balcony's structure). Plant climbing beans in deep troughs to train up trellis, or attach a sturdy wooden framework to the wall and nail on upcycled catering tins to make vertical gardens. Hook saddlebag planters over your railings, and fill hanging baskets from the ceiling dripping with strawberries, chillies or cherry tomatoes.

Just as for container gardens, patio varieties (see page 90) and shallow-rooted salads, greens and herbs are most successful on balconies. When you garden in the clouds, you're very exposed to the weather and conditions can get quite extreme, so match your crops carefully to your growing space and get ready to protect them from the worst.

South- or west-facing balconies are suntraps where heat lovers such as tomatoes, aubergines and chillies can bask in warmth. On shadier balconies, you'll be able to grow plenty of salads and leafy greens such as kale and chard, plus shade-loving herbs such as parsley, chervil and mint, and even alpine strawberries.

Plants can dry out quickly in the wind and sun, so keep on top of the watering – self-watering pots help keep the compost damp. Then have fun creating an oasis in the sky!

Bear in mind that balconies can be windy, so make sure your containers are stable and not top heavy, which would make them likely to fall over. Pots that are not secure risk being damaged or, worse still, they may fall over the edge and cause injury. Shelter can be created using a natural screen made of bamboo or wattle, for example.

Harvesting your crops

This is what it's all been for: that moment of pride and satisfaction when you know all the sowing, watering, fussing and fretting is behind you, your cherished plants are fully mature and bursting with health, and you can go gather in your harvest.

TIP

Tomatoes and strawberries keep developing sugars after they're harvested, so leave them at room temperature for a day or two before you eat them and they'll taste even better.

Time it right

How and when you harvest makes a big difference to the flavour and texture of your vegetables. One of the perks of growing your own is that you get to taste fruit and vegetables that have only just been picked – fresh food doesn't get any better. Time your harvest to perfection and salads are crunchy and tender, tomatoes and apples are perfectly ripe, and flavours and nutrients are at their peak.

Pick greens, herbs and salads in the early morning before the sun gets to them, so they're juicy with moisture. Tomatoes and most fruit are much better later in the day, when the sun has warmed their skins and developed the flavours.

Many vegetables taste best when they're young and tender. Pull beetroot and turnips once they're the size of a ping-pong ball, cut courgettes while they're no more than 15cm (6in) long and pick green beans while still smooth. Pick every few days to prompt your plants to keep producing more.

You'll need to make a judgement call on crops you want to ripen fully. Start testing sweetcorn cobs once the tassels turn brown – peel back the outer layer and pierce a kernel. You'll know it's just right when it oozes a milky liquid.

Squeeze cabbage heads to check they're firm before cutting them; leave the stumps in the ground and they'll resprout for an extra harvest of baby shoots.

Check ripening fruit every few days to watch the colour develop. Tomatoes, peppers, strawberries and melons max out on flavour and sweetness when they're fully coloured, and chillies are hotter when they're properly ripe, too. As soon as you're sure they've reached their peak, pick and enjoy.

Top: Leave onions to dry out on top of the soil for a few hours once they've been harvested.

Bottom: After harvesting, cabbages or lettuces will allow another harvest of small shoots.

Processing and storing

Mostly, you want your harvest to arrive steadily, with just enough to pick to fill your plates each day. But some crops deliver your harvest all at once, or in quantities you can't eat right away, so make the most of the bounty and stash what you can't immediately get through.

Gluts are often a good thing, giving you the chance to carry on enjoying homegrown food even when summer is a distant memory. In fact, it's often worth deliberately growing more than you need to guarantee full stores for winter.

Storage solutions

Freeze broad beans, French and runner beans, berries and peas. Lay broad beans, berries and peas in a single layer on a tray, freeze overnight, then decant into freezer bags. Blanch beans in boiling water for a couple of minutes, then dunk in iced water to cool before freezing whole.

Dry store apples, pears, marrows, squash, pumpkins and potatoes. 'Cure' harvested squash by drying for two weeks in a sunny greenhouse. Wrap apples and pears individually in newspaper, then pack into crates and store somewhere cool, airy and dry. Harvest maincrop potatoes in autumn, dry on the soil's surface for a few hours, then tip into hessian sacks and store somewhere dark.

Potatoes should be left to dry on the soil for a few hours in order to lose any excess moisture that might cause them to rot in storage.

GO GREENER

If you can't process all you grow, pass it on; apps such as Olio help eliminate food waste and tackle food poverty by advertising your surplus food for others to collect.

Pack in sand beetroot, turnips and celeriac. These crops are prone to frost damage and can turn unappetizingly woody if you leave them in the ground through winter, so lift in autumn, twist off the foliage and pack between layers of damp sand in crate.

Leave in the ground carrots and parsnips, covered with cardboard and straw. They are tough enough to survive and actually taste better because of it.

Dry tomatoes, chilli peppers, beans and peas. Thread chillies onto strong cotton and hang by a sunny window to dry. Cut tomatoes in half, dry in the sunshine for two weeks, (perhaps best on a sunny windowsill), then store in an airtight container in the fridge or in jars of olive oil.

Batch cook courgettes, aubergines, tomatoes, rhubarb and apples. Make ratatouille and pasta sauce from courgettes and aubergines and freeze for homegrown ready meals. Roughly chop tomatoes, rhubarb or apples, cook until soft and freeze in recipe-sized portions.

More glut-busting ideas

Chutney – courgettes, onions, green tomatoes and rhubarb.

Smoothies – carrot, beetroot, kale and cucumber.

Ferment – white cabbage, carrots and cucumbers.

Save your own seed

Once you've gathered everything in, there's one more harvest to collect and it may be the most important of them all.

Collect seed from your fruit, vegetables and herbs and you have all you need for next season's vegetable growing. It's free, and it's the most sustainable seed you'll ever sow – home-saved seed is organic, requires no plastic packaging or transport, and it's as local as it gets. Save from parent plants already thriving in your garden and their offspring are likely to flourish there, too.

To save your own seed, the parent plants must be open-pollinated varieties, bred through natural selection. Varieties with 'F1' on the seed packet are specially produced hybrids, bred for defined qualities such as disease resistance, and their offspring won't always be the same as the parents. Fruit, vegetables and herbs without F1 after the name are open pollinated – so you can safely save their seed and expect the next generation to be true, but only if there are no closely related varieties growing nearby.

Good genes make for a flourishing vegetable patch, so pick your star plants to save seed from. Look out for particularly fine specimens – perhaps they're particularly high yielding, slower to bolt or hold out longer against disease. Then mark your hero plants with coloured wool so you don't accidentally harvest all your would-be seeds!

Lettuces, beans and peas are mostly self-fertile, so you don't need any particular precautions to avoid cross-pollination, and that means saving their seed is very straightforward. Start off with these four, then have a go at saving seed from other crops as you feel ready.

The simplest way to save seed from crops that do cross-pollinate – such as brassicas or beetroot – is just to let one variety flower at a time. If that's not possible, you may have to physically isolate your plants, or hand pollinate (see overleaf).

Seed is ready to collect when fruits are so ripe they're all but dropping off the plant; seedheads and pods turn from green to nut-brown. Collect on a dry day and lay them somewhere sunny indoors to dry fully before processing.

Top: Clean and prepare seeds carefully before storing.

Bottom: Wait until seeds are fully ripe before harvesting.

GO GREENER

Allow several plants to flower rather than just one and collect a few seeds from all of them to be sure of good genetic diversity and guarantee the qualities you want are still there in the offspring.

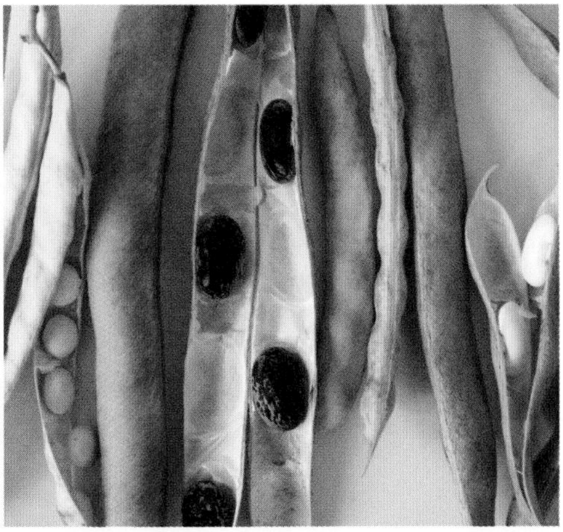

Seed-saving techniques

Each kind of crop demands a slightly different approach when it comes to saving its seed – you'll find specific instructions for each type on the pages that follow.

Hone your seed-saving skills further by mastering a few useful techniques to make sure you store your home-saved seed in good condition – and keep it that way until the day you come to sow it.

Collecting and storing

Podding and drying Once bean and pea pods turn yellow or brown, shuck out the seeds inside. Spread them across a tray and place in a sunny conservatory, spare room or greenhouse to finish drying for another week before storing.

Winnowing and threshing Chaff and debris turns mouldy in storage, so once you collect seedheads, carefully separate out or 'clean' the seed. Rub off the seeds as far as possible into a bucket and pick out larger debris by hand. Next, pass through a fine garden sieve a few times to remove more debris. Finally, pour seed plus chaff from one bucket to another outside on a breezy day; the chaff should blow away, leaving clean seed behind.

Isolation cages Peppers and chillies, plus chard, beetroot and spinach, are self-fertile, but insects can also cross-pollinate them. Keep seed true by physically isolating three or four plants as they start flowering under a cage made from second-hand cotton bedsheets or PLA (plastic-free cornstarch) insect-proof mesh, to keep insects out and the variety pure.

Storing seed Once your seed is thoroughly dried, tip it into paper envelopes marked with the variety and the date it was collected. Store somewhere dry and cool – most home-saved seed should keep for several years.

Hand pollinating

Prevent squashes cross-fertilizing with other varieties by hand pollinating.

- Find a female flower bud – with a baby fruit behind it – that's flushed yellow and just about to open, and gently tie it shut with wool.
- Next day, find a male flower (with a straight stem) and remove the petals to expose the central stamens.
- Remove the wool from your female flower bud, dab the male flower inside and move it about to transfer the pollen across.
- Tie the female flower closed again and mark it with a piece of wool tied around the stem behind the flower, so you know which fruit to save your seed from!

GREENER GARDENING: VEGETABLES // PART 3

Vegetables to grow

The range of fruit, vegetables and herbs you can grow in your back garden is mouthwatering. Everything is possible: humble spuds and cabbages, summery beans and courgettes, and expensive luxuries such as asparagus, melons and mangetout peas. You'll discover a whole new world of flavours you can't find in the shops, too: golden beetroot, fresh edamame beans, broad bean tops and lemony Chinese artichokes. And all of it is organic, plastic-free and with food miles measured in metres. Before you plunge in, though, plan your planting carefully to make sure there's something to pick every day of the year. Life in your kitchen is about to get a whole lot more interesting!

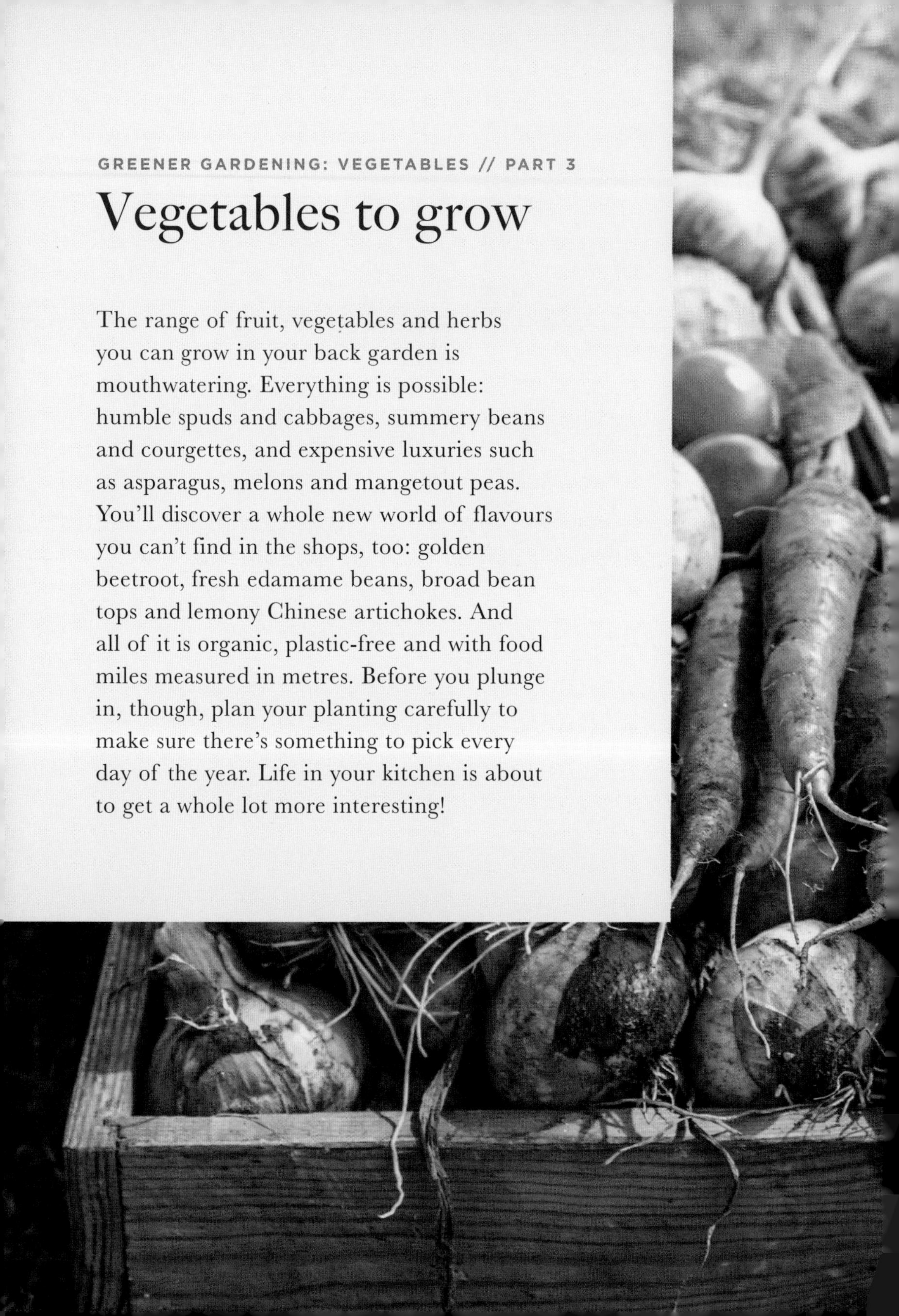

Year-round crops

There's a really useful group of crops that you can grow at any time of year, so you can guarantee picking some very nearly every day if you want to. These staples are great food security against those times when seasonal crops are in a bit of a lull, like that spell in early spring when there's lots growing, but little ready to harvest.

Resow leafy greens at regular intervals through the year and one crop takes over from another like a relay race – just switch to hardier winter varieties for growing through the coldest weather. Plant evergreen herbs and you'll never go short of aromatic flavours to pep up your cooking.

Perennial crops are the most rewarding of all (see pages 116–117). Plant once and they keep on giving year after year, all but guaranteeing you at least some homegrown food for your plate. They're also among the greenest crops you can grow, as you don't have to use up precious resources resowing them every year; they just stay in the ground, sequestering carbon and protecting the soil's ecosystem while giving you harvest after harvest for years.

TIP

Some seasonal crops like potatoes and beans are considered to be year-round staples because they store so well: keep potatoes in thick paper sacks and beans too if they are dried.

Lettuce

Salads aren't just for summer – lettuces grow year-round. Resow regularly, and switch to winter varieties to grow under glass barn cloches or in a cool greenhouse through cold weather. Have fun trying out the kaleidoscope of colours and shapes available, from crisp cos to soft butterheads.

SOWING

- Sow into wooden seed trays or newspaper modules under cover, in a cool greenhouse or on a bright windowsill.
- Prick out seedlings into 10cm (4in) pots at about 7cm (3in) tall.
- For baby-leaf salads, sow generously into large (35–45cm; 14–18in) containers.
- Resow monthly, switching to winter varieties in late summer. Sow one last batch in late autumn under cover and the seedlings overwinter, bursting into life for early spring harvests.

PLANTING

- Lettuce likes cool and damp, so choose a spot in part shade or plant between taller plants.
- Harden off carefully (see page 52) and plant outside or into roomy containers, 10–15cm (4–6in) apart.

CARE

- Keep well-watered or leaves turn bitter and plants may bolt.
- Shade beneath tunnels of wire hoops covered with thin cotton bedsheets on hot days.

TROUBLESHOOTING

- Protect seedlings against slugs; as they get older, they can withstand a little damage.
- Leaves can go mouldy when plants are too close or overwatered, especially in winter.
- Water well and keep shaded to prevent bolting in hot weather.

HARVESTING

- Snip baby leaves away at 7–10cm (3–4in) tall; they'll resprout several times before they're spent.
- Pick individual leaves while young, or cut whole heads once hearts are firm.

SAVING SEED

- Lettuces are highly self-fertile so there is no need to worry about different varieties crossing with each other.
- Have two or three of your best plants flowering for good genetic diversity.
- Once most of the seeds turn brown, cut the whole head to finish drying indoors.
- Winnow away the chaff from the seed (see page 102) and store in labelled paper envelopes.

Three to try

1. **'Merveille des Quatre Saisons'** Year-round, bronze-tinted leaves
2. **'Black-seeded Simpson'** Hefty and delicious for winter
3. **'Little Gem'** Classic mini-cos

GO GREENER

Growing loose-leaf varieties makes best use of resources as you harvest leaf by leaf over a longer period rather than cutting the whole head at once.

Kale

There's a kale for every season: tender Russian kales in summer; smoky Tuscan kales for autumn; and hardy kales for winter. There's even a kale with sweet, asparagus-like spears in spring.

SOWING AND GROWING

- Sow in late spring into newspaper modules (see page 51).
- Or sow direct into a well-prepared seedbed outdoors, thinning seedlings to leave the strongest.
- Transplant young plants to their final growing positions at 10–15cm (4–6in) tall, with the lowest leaves just at soil level.
- To grow baby leaf kale, sprinkle seed generously along a shallow drill or directly into a container.

TROUBLESHOOTING

- Grow under cages of PLA (plastic-free cornstarch) insect-proof mesh to fend off caterpillars and pigeons.
- In acidic soil add calcified seaweed three months before planting out.

HARVESTING

- Pick kale leaves young and tender.
- Snip baby kale leaves at 7–10cm (3–4in) tall, cutting just above ground level.
- Harvest asparagus kale spears at 10–15cm.

SAVING SEED

- As for Brussels sprouts (see page 162).

Three to try

1. **'Dwarf Green Curled'** Super-hardy, deeply crinkled leaves
2. **'Black Tuscany'** Strappy near-black leaves
3. **'Asparagus'** Sweet spring flower stem

Chard

Chard is drought tolerant, unfussy and resilient, making it an ideal choice for climate-changed gardens. Pick leaf by leaf and the harvest lasts weeks; cook the green leaf like spinach, and slice the brightly coloured midribs to steam or stir-fry.

SOWING AND GROWING

- Sow direct outside or into roomy containers, spacing seeds about 5cm (2in) apart.
- Make three sowings: one in spring, one in early summer and a final one in early autumn for a continuous supply, switching to hardier, white-stemmed varieties for winter harvests.
- Water young seedlings, chard growing in pots and mature plants in very dry spells.
- Chard is very hardy, but to keep leaves undamaged, cover with cloches in very bad weather.

TROUBLESHOOTING

- Chard suffers from very few problems – even the seedlings are rarely eaten by slugs, but if they are, raise them under cover in a cool greenhouse.

SAVING SEED

- As for beetroot (see page 142).

Three to try

1. **'Rhubarb chard'** Brilliant scarlet midribs
2. **'Swiss chard'** Hardiest in winter
3. **'Fordhook Giant'** Super-productive heirloom

Microgreens

When you need a quick burst of nutritious, intensely flavoured fresh salad leaves, any time of year, wherever you happen to be, sow microgreens. This is the ultimate in fast food – you can expect a harvest within a week or two, and they're so versatile you can grow them even if all you have is a windowsill.

SOWING

- Place a layer of peat-free multipurpose compost in the bottom of a recycled takeaway container or food tub and dampen with water.
- Scatter seeds generously over the compost. Lightly cover with more compost.
- You can also grow on a kitchen towel – fold it to fit the container, lay it in the bottom and dampen thoroughly before sowing on top.
- Sow more trays every couple of weeks for a constant supply.

CARE

- Keep on a bright windowsill or on a shelf in a cool greenhouse.
- Water gently using a mister or hand-spray.
- Peashoots are larger and thirstier and can be watered normally, with a small watering can.

TROUBLESHOOTING

- Microgreens are generally trouble-free as they're so fast-growing.
- Rotate trays by a quarter every day so seedlings don't lean towards the light and grow too spindly.

GO GREENER

Home-saved seeds make great edible microgreens, too, and they're plastic- and pesticide-free. However, make sure your seeds are very clean as microgreens are often eaten raw.

- If your seedlings turn mouldy or die suddenly (known as 'damping off'), you're probably overwatering; keep just damp to the touch, rather than wet.

HARVESTING

- Snip microgreens once the first pair of leaves are fully open – usually at 5–7cm (2–3in) tall.
- They should continue sprouting once or twice more, so don't clear the tray until you're sure they're spent.

Which microgreens?

Sow any kind of organic herb or vegetable seed and you'll get microgreens, so experiment with your favourite vegetables – the only ones off-limit are parsnips, which are poisonous at seedling stage. Harvesting so young intensifies flavours to the max, so vegetables with punchy, distinctive flavours, such as fennel, rocket, basil, coriander and sunflower, tend to make the best microgreens.

Three to try

1. **Red basil** Deliciously nutty purple sprouts
2. **Radish** Lightly peppery and crunchy
3. **Coriander** Spicy, fresh flavour

Evergreen herbs

Evergreen herbs are the most accommodating of plants. They take up very little room for all the fistfuls of fragrant, spicily aromatic leaves they provide; one or two plants are usually enough, and they'll grow happily in containers. They're long-lived and, best of all, you can pick them every day – even in the depths of winter.

SOWING

- Larger evergreen herbs such as rosemary, sage and bay grow slowly and may take years to reach picking size if sown from seed, so grow from cuttings or buy young plants from a peat-free, organic herb supplier.
- Sow thyme and winter savory in spring into newspaper modules filled with peat-free seed compost.

CARE

- Plant in gritty, free-draining soil in your sunniest spot. Add grit or sand to the compost if growing in containers.
- After flowering, cut foliage back by about half to keep plants compact.

TROUBLESHOOTING

- Rosemary beetles attack thyme and sage as well as rosemary; the shiny metallic purple beetles feed on leaves and flowers. They rarely cause serious harm, though - natural predators should control populations, so encourage a good biodiversity in your garden.

Three to try

1. **Rosemary** Tall, elegant shrub
2. **Thyme** Common thyme (*Thymus vulgaris*) is most productive
3. **Bay** Keep clipped to a manageable size

- All evergreen herbs hate being too damp, so be careful not to overwater, and if your soil is heavy or poorly drained, grow in containers instead.
- Plants can become leggy and less productive after a few years; take cuttings to make new plants and replace the old ones.

GO GREENER

Plant evergreen herbs among other vegetables as natural deterrents for undesirables - the herbs' pungent scents confuse and put off insects from flea beetles to aphids.

Herbal houseplants

Root evergreen lemongrass stems for year-round citrussy flavouring to use in Thai dishes and teas.

- Buy stems of lemongrass in spring and pop them in a glass of water on a sunny windowsill.
- Change the water every few days and in three or four weeks you should see roots forming.
- Pot up rooted stems in containers of compost.
- Grow in containers – keep them outside in summer, then bring into the house to keep them warm through winter. They make good houseplants for a sunny windowsill.

Perennial vegetables

Sowing vegetables from scratch every year is resource hungry and time-consuming – so don't! Focus on vegetables that come back year after year and all you have to do, apart from a little light maintenance, is gather the harvest. You'll do your soil a favour, too, as perennial vegetables help protect soil ecosystems and lock away carbon.

FIVE FOREVER FOODS

'Daubentons' kale Tall perennial kale with nutritious, hearty, purple-tinged leaves.

- Propagate only from cuttings (from heirloom vegetable plant suppliers); root in pots of damp, gritty compost.
- Cover with PLA (plastic-free cornstarch) insect-proof mesh in summer against pigeons and butterflies.
- Stake plants when fully grown.
- Pick leaves no more than 10cm (4in) long, year-round, for up to five years.

'Nine Star' broccoli About 1m (3ft) tall, with tasty white florets like mini-cauliflowers.

- Sow seed into newspaper modules filled with peat-free compost in spring.
- Pot seedlings on as they grow, then harden off and plant outside 45cm (18in) apart.
- Protect with PLA (plastic-free cornstarch) insect-proof mesh.
- Cut the central, larger floret first, then harvest smaller florets; they keep coming for about three years.

Jerusalem artichokes Nutty, hearty underground tubers to harvest all winter.

- Bury tubers 15cm (6in) deep and 30cm (12in) apart in free-draining soil in sun or part shade.
- Support plants loosely with hazel or bamboo and string; Jerusalem artichokes grow up to 3m (10ft) tall.
- Dig up tubers as required from late autumn – leave some in the ground to regrow for next year's crop.

Caucasian spinach
Lush hardy climber – harvest young leaves like spinach.

- Place seeds in a bag of damp compost and leave in the fridge for 10 days, then sow into a 10cm (4in) pot in spring. Move seedlings into their own containers once big enough to handle.
- Give plants sturdy hazel wigwams or trellis to scramble up.
- Leave to grow for the first year, then harvest young shoots and leaves from spring.

Skirret Carrot-like clusters of skinny roots with a sweet flavour.

- Buy one-year-old crowns, or place seeds in a bag of damp compost and leave in the fridge for 10 days before sowing direct into rich soil in a sunny spot.
- Keep well-watered and leave to grow for the first year.
- Dig up clumps in autumn, remove larger roots to eat, then replant for next year's crops.
- Clean roots, then eat raw or pan-fry in butter.

More to try

Chinese artichokes (crosnes), **rhubarb**, **asparagus** (see page 120) and **Welsh onions** (see page 147).

Vegetables to grow in spring: essential tasks

Gardeners are an optimistic bunch – and never more so than in spring, when the sunshine is warm and you can start sowing again. But this is also hungry gap time, when vegetable stores are dwindling and there's little to pick, so make space for those few vegetables at their peak right now to keep the harvest coming.

- **Put up plant supports** Build wigwams and A-frame supports for beans, peas and taller maincrop peas.
- **Dig in green manures** Shear off top growth, then dig plants back into the soil to release their nutrients.
- **Start hoeing weekly** Weeds start growing fast now, so run a hoe over beds once a week.
- **Make a nursery bed** Nursery beds are great for direct sowing brassicas and leeks away from summer crops to transplant later. Choose a sunny spot and rake off stones ready to sow.
- **Start patrolling for slugs and snails** Check vulnerable plants such as newly emerging seedlings daily. The best time to patrol for them is just after sunset, or at night on damp evenings.
- **Sow annual flowers** Dot cornflowers, pot marigolds and nasturtiums among vegetables to attract pollinators.
- **Lift and divide clump-forming herbs** Dig up marjoram, mint and chives (after flowering) and split to make new plants.
- **Harvest rhubarb** Do this by pulling stems gently away from the crown.

Asparagus

Asparagus demands very few resources in return for the fistfuls of succulent, tender spears it produces every spring for years, so it's a great crop for sustainable, low-impact gardens.

SOWING AND GROWING

- Plant in sun or part shade, in very free-draining soil; if yours is heavy, plant into raised beds.
- To plant crowns, make trenches 30cm (12in) deep, heap up soil along the bottom, spread out crowns over this ridge 30cm apart, then backfill.
- It's usually more sustainable to grow organically from seed; sow in early spring, in newspaper modules, and transplant outside in early summer.
- Wait two years before harvesting for crowns, three for seed-raised asparagus.
- Support the tall stems through summer – once they yellow in autumn, cut away to ground level.

TROUBLESHOOTING

- Weed by hand to avoid damaging roots.
- Remove female berrying plants.
- Pick off asparagus beetles that eat foliage.

SAVING SEED

- Collect ripe, red berries in late summer.
- Remove seeds, rinse and dry before storing.

Three to try

1. **'Mary Washington'** Thick, purple-flushed spears
2. **'Connover's Colossal'** Early-maturing and prolific
3. **'Gijnlim'** Modern all-male variety

TIP

Get the most from your harvest by cutting every other plant as loose greens, leaving the rest to heart up for a later, second crop of full-sized cabbages.

Spring cabbage

Timing is everything when growing spring cabbage – you want plants big enough by early winter to produce lush heads of sweet greens in early spring, but not so big that they're past their best.

SOWING AND GROWING

- Sow in mid- to late summer into 5cm (2in) newspaper modules filled with peat-free seed compost.
- Make another 'insurance' sowing one month later in case a warm autumn brings seedlings on too fast.
- Transplant seedlings outside once 10cm (4in) tall, spaced 10cm apart, and firm in well, or sow direct outside, 5cm apart.
- Give mature plants a post-winter boost with a liquid seaweed feed in early spring.
- In acidic soil add lime about three months before planting.

TROUBLESHOOTING

- Grow under cages of PLA (plastic-free cornstarch) insect-proof mesh to fend off cabbage white butterflies and pigeons.

SAVING SEED

- As for Brussels sprouts (see page 162).

Three to try

1. **'April'** Compact and reliable
2. **'Offenham 2'** Classic pointed heads
3. **'Spring Hero'** Hardy, with rounded heads

Purple sprouting broccoli

Purple sprouting broccoli is a spring treat you'll look forward to all year. You won't need many plants as they're tall, hefty and prolifically generous, sending out a steady supply of deliciously sweet and tender sultry purple florets to see you comfortably through the hungry gap.

SOWING

- Scatter a pinch of seed into 10cm (4in) clay pots full of dampened multipurpose compost in mid-spring and keep on a windowsill or in a cool greenhouse to germinate.
- Once seedlings are large enough to handle, gently tip them out and split apart to pot up in their own containers.
- You can also sow direct outside into drills in a finely raked seedbed. Remove the smallest seedlings to leave the largest to grow on.

PLANTING

- Once seedlings are about 10cm tall, plant outside into rich soil in a sunny spot, leaving 60cm (24in) between plants and firming them in well.
- Purple sprouting broccoli grows very slowly and won't mature until winter, so sow summer crops such as lettuces or beetroot in between the plants to make best use of the space.

CARE

- Water young seedlings regularly; once mature, only water in dry spells.
- Stake plants firmly in autumn against winter gales.

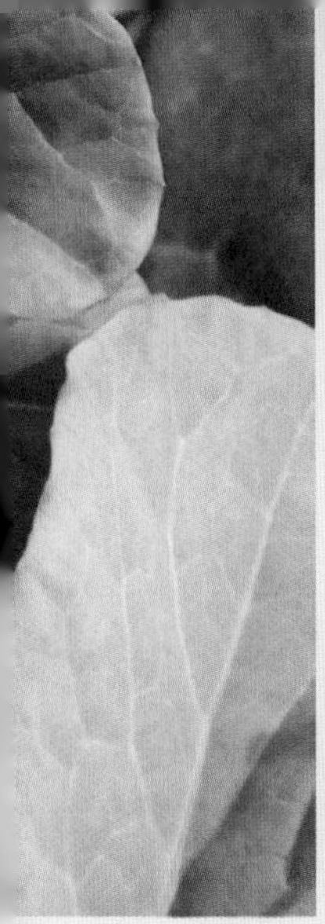

TROUBLESHOOTING

- In very acidic soil add calcified seaweed three months before planting out.
- Cover with a cage of PLA (plastic-free cornstarch) insect-proof mesh as soon as you plant outside to keep cabbage white caterpillars and pigeons off your plants.

HARVESTING

- Once florets are fully coloured – but still tightly in bud – cut them away from the stem with about 10cm of stem and leaves (these can all be eaten).
- Florets will keep coming for several weeks, so keep coming back to pick more!

SAVING SEED

- As for Brussels sprouts (see page 162).

GO GREENER

Avoid a wasteful glut by sowing a mix of varieties maturing at different rates to eke out your harvest – the earliest are ready in late winter, and the latest keep you picking until late spring/ early summer.

Three to try

1. **'Rudolph'** Super-early and productive
2. **'Claret'** Late-spring harvests
3. **'Early Purple Sprouting'** Classic mid-season performer

Vegetables to grow in summer: essential tasks

As summer finally bursts into its full joyous glory, there is simply no better place to be than the vegetable garden. It's a busy time – as well as keeping up with picking all that lovely produce, you're planting up your vegetable beds, holding back the weeds and staying on top of watering.

- **Keep sowing** Sow batches of lettuces and other salads, plus beetroot, turnips, kohl rabi and carrots every month right through until late summer for a continuous supply.
- **Watch perennial weeds** Pull away or hoe off top growth from perennial weeds once a week to keep them in check.
- **Encourage wildflowers** Let a few less troublesome 'weeds' (aka wildflowers) self-seed among your vegetables to attract pollinating insects.
- **Pick regularly** Harvest courgettes and climbing beans twice weekly so you catch them at prime picking size and plants stay productive.
- **Tie in climbers** Tie in climbing plants to supports using jute or hessian twine.
- **Train your tomatoes** Pinch out sideshoots on tomatoes every few days, as shown left.
- **Water wisely** Save 'grey' water from baths and washing-up bowls (use eco-friendly detergents) to use on the garden.
- **Add homemade liquid feed** Add this feed to the watering can weekly when feeding crops in containers or in the greenhouse.

Peas

You'll know you've arrived as a vegetable gardener when you find yourself popping open a pod of sweet, plump peas to snack on while you do the watering. Homegrown peas are superb, and a real summer treat – just make sure you grow lots of them so at least some make it back to the kitchen!

SOWING AND GROWING

- Sow five seeds to a 10cm (4in) pot of peat-free multipurpose compost from early spring (don't sow direct outdoors as pea seeds are caviar to mice and slugs). Keep on a bright windowsill or in a cool greenhouse until they germinate.
- Sow a second batch of mangetout and early peas (but not maincrops) in midsummer to keep picking into autumn.

PLANTING: PODDING PEAS

- Harden off ready for planting out once seedlings are 8–10cm (3–4in) tall.
- Put up strong wigwams or A-frames made of hazel for tall maincrop varieties to climb, then plant one potful of seedlings at each leg of the support.
- Tie the stems into their supports regularly as they grow.
- Plant potfuls of early peas 15cm (6in) apart – these are shorter, so need less support. Poke twiggy hazel pea sticks between plants for them to scramble up, or grow them up netting.

PLANTING: MANGETOUT PEAS

- Stretch jute netting between 1m-tall (3ft) hazel sticks poked into the ground at 1m intervals along the row. Plant potfuls of peas 15cm apart along the base.
- Tuck tendrils into the netting as they grow.

CARE

- Water young seedlings, and mature plants once they're flowering.

TROUBLESHOOTING

- Mice eat newly sown seeds and just-emerged seedlings, so sow under cover out of harm's way.
- Pea moth larvae sometimes eat peas inside the pods – you'll only find the damage at harvest time. A few are tolerable but if they're problematic, grow under PLA (plastic-free cornstarch) insect-proof mesh.

HARVESTING

- Pick podding peas while still smooth – hold the pod up to the light (still on the plant) to check whether the peas inside are fully developed.
- You can also harvest peashoots from plants as they grow.
- Harvest mangetouts young, while the pods are still flat.

SAVING SEED

- As for climbing beans (see overleaf).

Three to try

1. **'Magnum Bonum'** Tall, prolifically generous Victorian heirloom
2. **'Oregon Sugar Pod'** Masses of delicious mangetouts
3. **'Douce Provence'** Early crops on compact plants

Climbing and dwarf beans

Summer wouldn't be summer without the sweet, crisp flavour of green beans. They're super-easy to grow – choose from pencil-thin French beans, or prolifically generous flat-podded runners, then extend the season with dwarf beans plus dried shelling beans for winter.

SOWING

- Sow in late spring, 2cm (1in) deep into saved cardboard toilet roll inners (see page 49) filled with homemade or peat-free multipurpose compost.
- Sow a second batch of dwarf beans in late summer to keep picking into autumn.
- After the last frost, acclimatize seedlings to outdoor conditions by leaving them out longer each day for 10 to 14 days.
- French and dwarf beans, and compact runner bean 'Hestia', also grow well in large containers – sow seeds direct, about 15cm (6in) apart.

PLANTING: CLIMBING BEANS

- Build a 2m-tall (7ft) wigwam from five to six hazel rods sunk into the ground, then tied firmly together with jute twine.
- Plant two plants at the foot of each leg.

PLANTING: DWARF (BUSH) BEANS

- Plant in blocks, 15cm apart each way.
- Poke hazel or birch twigs into the ground among plants for support.

CARE

- Tie climbing bean stems into supports with jute twine as they grow.

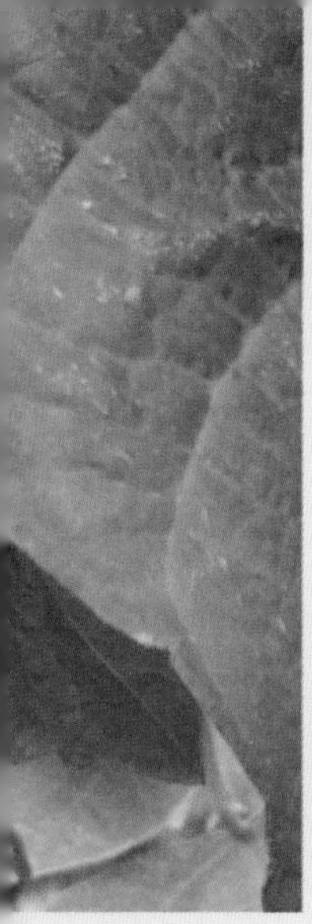

GO GREENER

Once you finish harvesting your beans, cut away spent growth and add to the compost heap – but leave roots in the ground to rot naturally and boost your soil with carbon.

- Water container-grown beans daily in dry weather. In the open garden, water with saved rainwater or grey water only if there's dry weather as flowers appear.

TROUBLESHOOTING

- Tolerate small numbers of blackfly – they're essential food for predators such as ladybirds. Blast larger numbers off with water using a hose on jet setting.

SAVING SEED

- French beans are great for beginner seed savers as they're self-fertile, so the second generation come back the same as the parents, and the seeds don't need cleaning.
- Mark your best plants with coloured wool so you remember not to pick your seeds.
- Once mature pods turn yellow, harvest them and shuck out the seeds.
- Spread out on a tray to finish drying somewhere warm and dry for a fortnight.

Shelling beans

For dried beans to use in hearty winter stews and soups, leave all pods on the plant, then harvest in autumn. Follow the instructions for saving seed (left), and store in glass jars. Soak overnight, then boil rapidly for 10 minutes before using.

Three to try

1. **'Cherokee Trail of Tears'** Jet-black beans perfect for chilli dishes
2. **'Czar'** Fat white beans, treated like butter beans
3. **'Blue Lake'** Delicate white haricots

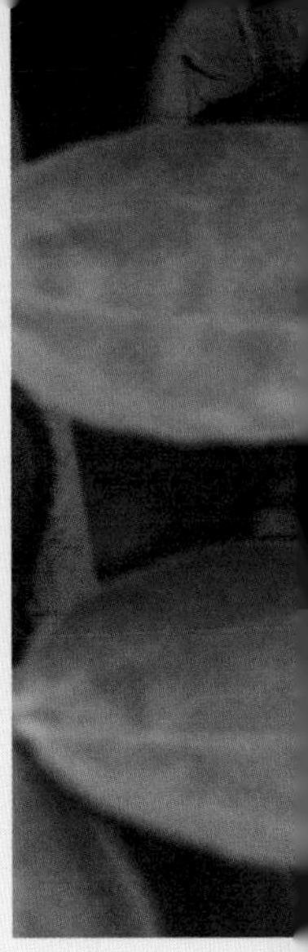

Broad beans

Sturdy, reliable and easy to grow, broad beans are among the first homegrown harvests of the new season. Overwinter hardy varieties to give them a head start and you'll pick sweet, tender baby beans by early summer.

SOWING

- Sow into saved toilet roll inners filled with peat-free multipurpose (ideally homemade) compost in mid-autumn for overwintering (hardier varieties only), or in early spring.
- Germinate seeds indoors, then move outside to continue growing; seedlings grow sappy and weak if kept too warm.

PLANTING

- Plant overwintered seedlings into their final growing spaces in early spring, 10–15cm (4–6in) apart.
- Spring-sown seedlings can be planted out as soon as they're 8–10cm (3–6in) tall.
- Broad beans generally support each other, but put canes and string around the outside of the row to keep outer plants from falling over.

CARE

- Water young seedlings and mature plants once they're flowering.

TROUBLESHOOTING

- Mice adore newly sown broad bean seeds, so sow under cover out of harm's way.
- Blackfly attack plants from midsummer – overwintered broad beans escape the worst. Blast larger numbers off with water using a hose on jet setting, and remove the sappy top growth where blackfly tends to cluster in early summer once pods have formed.

TIP

If you miss some pods and the beans inside are overmature, instead of throwing them out, cook for 10 minutes, slip off their skins and whizz with garlic, oil and lemon juice to make broad bean hummus.

- The fungal disease chocolate spot causes brown spots on the leaves from midsummer onwards on spring-sown beans and can seriously weaken plants. Space plants further apart to improve air circulation.

HARVESTING

- Pick pods once you feel beans swelling inside.
- You can also harvest the tops once pods have set. Snip off the top 15cm (6in) just above a leaf.

SAVING SEED

- As for climbing beans (see page 129) but broad beans will cross-pollinate with other varieties grown in the general area.

Growing edamame

Scrummy, protein-packed green edamame (soya) beans are great stir-fried or served with sushi, and you grow them just like broad beans. Choose cool-climate varieties such as 'Elena', and sow in mid-spring, planting outside after the last frost. Each pod contains two or three delicious beans.

Three to try

1. **'Aquadulce Claudia'** Super-hardy for overwintering
2. **'The Sutton'** Compact and thrives in containers
3. **'Imperial Green Longpod'** Massive pods and high yields

Courgettes and other summer squash

Courgettes are legendary for their generosity – expect to pick three or four sweet, tender fruits every few days. They're just one of a kaleidoscope of summer squashes you can try when you grow your own, from scalloped patty pans to skittle-shaped crooknecks.

SOWING

- You only need two or three plants – they're big (at least 1m; 3ft across) and each will produce fruit in prolific quantities.
- Sow seeds in late spring, burying them 1cm (0.4in) deep in a 10cm (4in) clay pot of dampened, peat-free multipurpose compost.
- Keep warm, and once seedlings are big enough to handle, tip them out – gently tease them apart and repot into their own 10cm pots.

PLANTING

- Harden off (see page 52), then plant outside in a sunny spot in rich soil when all danger of frost has passed. Leave 90cm (35in) between plants.
- Water in well and mulch after planting.

CARE

- Water in dry spells, directing the flow at the base of the plant, as damp leaves are prone to mildew.
- Feed patio courgettes in containers weekly with comfrey tea once they're flowering.

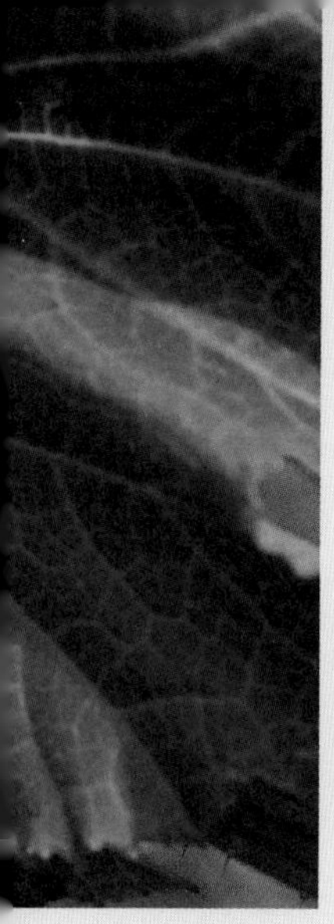

GO GREENER

Sink clay pots into the ground alongside each plant and fill each time you water, so the moisture drains slowly into the rootzone with not a drop lost to evaporation.

TROUBLESHOOTING

- Slugs raze new seedlings to the ground, so sow under cover and plant out only once plants are well developed.
- Early fruits can rot off without developing in cold spells, but this usually rights itself as the weather improves.
- Mildew is common in late summer, turning leaves powdery white and bringing harvesting to a premature end. Watering leaves with a 50:50 mix of milk and water from midsummer helps prevent this happening. Pick off affected leaves to slow the spread.

HARVESTING

- Cut fruits young, no more than 15cm (6in) long or wide.
- Harvest every few days – if you leave fruits to mature, the plant stops producing more.

SAVING SEED

- Follow hand-pollination instructions on page 103.
- Allow pollinated fruits to develop to full maturity.
- Then save seed as for winter squash (see page 153).

Three to try

1. **'Defender'** Super-reliable dark green courgettes
2. **'Sunburst'** Brilliant yellow patty pans
3. **'Zephyr'** Gorgeous two-tone crooknecks

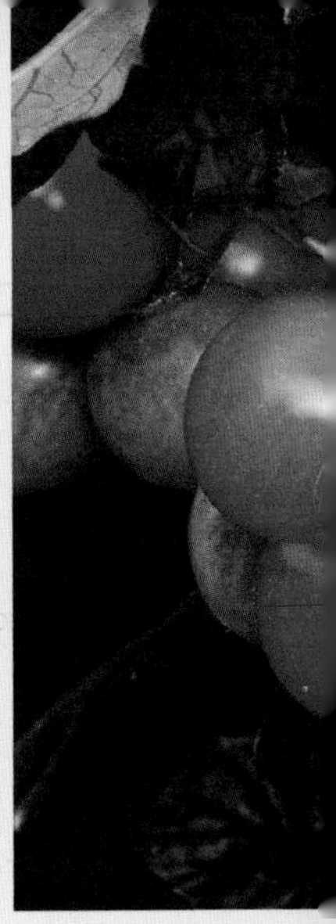

Tomatoes

Whatever garden you have – even if you have no garden at all – there's always room for tomatoes! A greenhouse helps ripen fruit and protects plants from blight – but blight-resistant varieties and longer, warmer summers let you grow tomatoes successfully outdoors, too.

SOWING

- Tomatoes are big, generous plants - so you'll only need a few! In early spring, fill a 10cm (4in) pot with peat-free compost, water, then space seeds evenly across the top. Cover with more compost.
- Keep on a windowsill indoors or in a heated propagator set to 18°C (64°F).
- Once seedlings are large enough to handle, tip them out, tease apart and repot into their own 10cm pots.
- Grow somewhere warm and bright, in a heated propagator or on a sunny windowsill.

PLANTING

- In early summer, harden off outdoor tomatoes, then plant into rich soil in a sunny spot 45–60cm (18–24in) apart, or into 35–45cm-diameter (14–18in) containers and hanging baskets. Plant deeply, so the bottom-most leaves are just above soil level.
- Plant greenhouse tomatoes straight into borders, homemade hessian grow bags or 35–45cm containers.

CARE

- Train tall cordon varieties by tying stems to a 2m (7ft) cane or hazel stick support. Remove all sideshoots.
- Bush varieties don't need training or support.

GO GREENER

Grow your own plant supports; common hazel produces ramrod straight stems when coppiced – harvest in early spring, at 3–5cm (1–2in) thick, to support tomatoes, beans and peas.

- Water regularly – daily in hot weather – and feed weekly with comfrey tea once plants flower.

TROUBLESHOOTING

- Late blight is carried in rain – greenhouse growing keeps foliage dry. Outside, grow blight-resistant varieties.
- Whitefly can be a nuisance in greenhouses, so plant French marigolds among plants and release the biological control *Encarsia formosa*.
- Blossom end rot causes blackened, corky lesions on fruits – it's caused by erratic watering.

SAVING SEED

- Choose a very ripe fruit, cut it in half and scoop out the seed and pith.
- Spread across a kitchen towel and dry for two weeks on a bright windowsill.
- Store in a paper envelope.
- In spring, lay the kitchen towel and seeds onto compost in a seed tray and cover with more compost for seedlings within about two weeks.

Three to try

1. **'Ailsa Craig'** Super-reliable classic red salad tomato
2. **'Marmande'** French beefsteak, outstanding flavour
3. **'Crimson Crush'** Blight-resistant variety with large, juicy fruit.

Cucumbers

The smooth, green cucumbers in shops are greenhouse cucumbers; outdoor cucumbers have warty skins, and include gherkins and cornichons for pickling.

SOWING AND GROWING

- In early spring (greenhouse cucumbers) or late spring (outdoor varieties), sow seeds 1cm (0.4in) deep in 10cm (4in) clay pots of compost and keep warm.
- In early summer, plant greenhouse cucumbers into borders or containers, and harden off outdoor cucumbers before planting in a sunny spot, 30cm (12in) apart. Provide canes or jute netting for plants to scramble up.
- Pinch out top shoots at 2m (7ft) tall, and non-fruiting sideshoots at 60cm (24in).

TROUBLESHOOTING

- Greenhouse cucumbers turn bitter if pollinated – remove male flowers (with straight stems).
- Red spider mite is worse in dry greenhouses; spritz with water to raise humidity. Remove dying leaves and release biological controls.

SAVING SEED

- Grow just one variety, or cover with an isolation cage and hand pollinate flowers. (Note: once pollinated, greenhouse cucumbers turn bitter and inedible.)

Three to try

1. **'Telegraph Improved'** Classic long greenhouse cucumber
2. **'Marketmore'** Prolific outdoor cropper
3. **'Crystal Lemon'** Round-fruited and delicious

Aubergines

Aubergines need sunshine, which can make them tricky to grow in cooler climates. But with ever-warmer summers, your chances of ripening a good crop – even outdoors – are improving.

SOWING AND GROWING

- Sow in early spring into newspaper modules in a propagator heated to 21°C (70°F). Pot on as they grow and keep warm.
- In early summer, plant into borders or 35–45cm (14–18in) containers in a greenhouse. Harden off outdoor aubergines and plant in your sunniest spot, 60cm (24in) apart.
- Tie plants to 30cm (12in) supports and remove shoot tips at 30cm to encourage branching.

TROUBLESHOOTING

- Flowers can drop without producing fruit in greenhouses – hand-pollinate by dabbing a soft paintbrush into each flower.
- Red spider mite (see cucumbers opposite) also affects aubergines.

SAVING SEED

- Let fruits mature to muddy-brown or yellow.
- Cut into quarters lengthwise, dunk into a bowl of water and rub out seeds.
- Let good seed sink to the bottom and filter off the debris. Rinse, then dry seeds before storing.

Three to try

1. **'Black Beauty'** Fat, dark and glossy
2. **'Long Purple'** Long, early fruits
3. **'Ivory' F1** Small, white fruits for containers

GO GREENER

Instead of heating a propagator, cover just-sown seeds in a clear plastic bag and pop in your airing cupboard. Check daily, and move to a warm, bright windowsill once germinated.

Sweet peppers

As well as classic, blocky bell peppers, homegrown sweet peppers come in curvy, round and snack-sized shapes, too. They need lots of warmth – you'll usually need a greenhouse for them to fruit well.

SOWING AND GROWING

- Sow in early spring into newspaper modules in a propagator heated to 21°C (70°F). Pot into larger containers as they grow, and keep warm.
- Plant into borders or 35–45cm (14–18in) containers in a greenhouse in late spring. Add a cane and tie in plants as they grow.
- Keep well-watered and feed weekly with comfrey feed once flowering.
- Pinch out top shoots at 30cm (12in) tall to encourage more fruits.

TROUBLESHOOTING

- Check shoot tips regularly and remove any aphids.
- Peppers also suffer from red spider mite (see cucumbers on page 136).

SAVING SEED

- As for chillies (see opposite)

Three to try

1. **'Gourmet'** Chunky orange bell pepper
2. **'Corno di Toro Rosso'** Richly flavoured, long and red
3. **'Diablo'** High yields of bull-horn-type fruits

TIP

Chillies develop their heat as they ripen, so wait until they colour fully for the full, mouth-blistering experience.

Chillies

When choosing chillies, how hot can you go? Superhots such as 'Carolina Reaper' can reduce the hardest chilli-heads to tears, but most are milder, with pretty fruit and rich flavours.

SOWING

- As for sweet peppers (see opposite).

GROWING

- Chillies fruit best in greenhouses, but also do well in containers on a sunny patio.
- In early summer, plant into 25cm (10in) containers and place in the greenhouse, or harden off carefully and place outside in full sun.
- Tie taller varieties to canes for support.
- Pinch out shoot tips once plants reach 30cm (12in) tall.
- Keep well-watered, and feed with comfrey feed once flowering.

TROUBLESHOOTING

- As for sweet peppers (see opposite).

SAVING SEED

- Grow just one variety or cover plants with isolation cages (see page 103).
- Once fruits are fully ripe, cut open and remove seeds (wear gloves for chillies).
- Dry for two weeks before storing.

Three to try

1. **'Scotch Bonnet'** Curiously shaped and hot
2. **'Rocoto'** Very tall, and cold tolerant
3. **'Basket of Fire'** Compact enough for hanging baskets

Carrots

Carrots pulled straight from the garden are richly flavoured and sweet – you can grow a steady supply right through the year, as well as extras for storing into winter.

SOWING

- Always sow carrots direct where they're to grow; if sowing into containers or in stony soils, opt for short- and round-rooted varieties.
- Make a shallow drill, water well, then sprinkle seeds sparingly along the bottom. Cover lightly with soil. Water daily until seedlings emerge.
- Sow a batch of fast-maturing early carrots every month for steady supplies through summer, adding a late-spring sowing of maincrops to mature slowly until autumn for winter stores.

CARE

- Remove every other seedling until plants are 5cm (2in) apart; as the seedlings you pull out get larger, you can eat them as tiny fingerling carrots.
- Water in prolonged dry weather.

TROUBLESHOOTING

- Carrot flies tunnel holes into roots, so grow resistant varieties, cover crops with PLA (plastic-free cornstarch) insect-proof mesh or put up a 60cm-high (24in) screen round them made out of second-hand cotton sheets.
- Roots often fork in stony or over-rich soil; avoid adding manure where you're planning to grow them, and grow round- or stump-rooted varieties if your soil has lots of stones in it.

HARVESTING

- Pull carrots young for the sweetest flavour – feel gently beneath the soil and when you find a root with 'shoulders' 2–3cm (0.8–1in) across, ease it out.
- Maincrop carrots can stay in the ground over winter but often keep growing, so become overmature. Lift in autumn and store in crates of damp sand instead (see page 99).

SAVING SEED

- Leave a row of 40 to 50 carrots in the ground over winter or replant stored carrots in spring – they'll burst into exuberant flower the following summer.
- Harvest fully ripe seedheads and dry further indoors, then rub off seeds, thresh out the debris and store.
- Discard any white roots you find when harvesting carrots grown from home-saved seed – these are the result of cross-pollination with wild carrots (Queen Anne's lace) and don't make good eating.

TIP

Grow straight carrots in stony soil by making a 30cm-deep (12in) hole with a crowbar; fill with a 50:50 mix of sand and sieved garden compost, and sow into the top.

Three to try

1. **'Flyaway'** Resistant to carrot fly
2. **'Amsterdam Forcing'** Reliable early variety
3. **'Autumn King'** Sturdy maincrop that stores well

Beetroot

Beetroot is easy to grow and a zero-food-waste vegetable – pick leaves for salads or cook like spinach, then pull the richly flavoured roots.

SOWING AND GROWING

- Sow seeds 2cm (0.8in) apart into pre-watered drills or containers. Thin seedlings to 10cm (4in) apart.
- Repeat sow monthly from spring until late summer for a continuous supply.
- Harvest at golf-ball size; in autumn, lift your last crop, twist off the tops and store packed in damp sand for winter eating.

TROUBLESHOOTING

- Slugs and mice eat seedlings, so sow under cover where they're safer.
- Plants bolt (run to seed) in very hot weather, so try bolt-resistant varieties.

SAVING SEED

- Beetroot cross-pollinates with chard or spinach beet, so let only one type flower.
- Plants only flower and set seed in their second summer, so leave roots in the ground at the end of the season.
- Stake the 1.5m-tall (5ft) flower spikes to keep them upright.
- Cut seedheads once brown and shake out the dark-coloured seeds.

Three to try

1. **'Boltardy'** Classic, dark purple beetroot with good bolting resistance
2. **'Burpees Golden'** Same flavour but without staining everything pink
3. **'Chioggia'** Slices into pink and white rings that look lovely raw in salads

Turnips

Homegrown turnips are a revelation – grown fast through summer, and harvested young, they're spicy, fresh and tender. Some are sweet enough to grate raw into salads.

SOWING AND GROWING

- Sow direct into sunny free-draining soil in the vegetable garden or 45cm-diameter (18in) containers.
- Scatter seeds thinly along a pre-watered shallow drill and cover with more soil.
- Remove weaker seedlings to leave the strongest 15cm (6in) apart to grow.
- Sow small quantities each month from spring until late summer for harvesting at ping-pong ball size - you can pick leaves, too, for richly flavoured turnip 'tops'.

TROUBLESHOOTING

- Flea beetles pepper seedling leaves with holes - grow under PLA (plastic-free cornstarch) insect-proof mesh from the start. This also protects against pigeons and cabbage white caterpillars.
- Plants bolt early if they go thirsty, so keep well-watered.

SAVING SEED

- Let only your best roots flower, then follow the same procedure as for sprouts (see page 162).

Three to try

1. **'Purple Top Milan'** Flattened purple-tinged roots
2. **'Golden Ball'** Neat golden globes
3. **'Tokyo Cross'** Fast growing and sweet

Potatoes

The nation's favourite vegetable is a great crop for beginners. Explore the full range, from purple heritage varieties to Maya 'phureja' types – there's always a new one to try!

SOWING

- Chit new (first early) potatoes in egg cartons, letting them sprout before planting.
- Plant new potatoes first, in mid-spring, then second earlies two weeks later, and finally maincrops.
- Make 15cm-deep (6in) holes with a trowel, 30cm (12in) apart for new potatoes and 45cm (18in) apart for the rest. Drop in a seed potato and backfill.

CARE

- Pull up earth over emerging stems with a hoe, or avoid disturbing the soil and simply bury with garden compost to prevent green potatoes and encourage more tubers to form.
- Water in dry weather.

TROUBLESHOOTING

- Frost damage turns newly emerged foliage brown, so plant later, or protect with glass barn cloches.
- Late blight can turn plants to mush in late summer. First and second earlies aren't usually affected – if growing maincrops, stick to blight-resistant maincrop varieties.

HARVESTING

- Ten to 12 weeks after planting, dig up your harvest carefully without spearing tubers with your fork.
- For harvesting maincrop potatoes to store, see page 99.

GO GREENER

Avoid disturbing the soil's delicate ecosystem by burying seed potatoes shallowly in thick mulch spread across the soil's surface. Heap compost, grass clippings or straw over stems as they grow, then simply pull up the plants - spuds and all - to harvest without having to dig.

SAVING SEED

- Commercially grown organic seed potatoes are certified virus-free and safest, but you can also save your own. If the crop deteriorates, though, start again with bought stock.
- Harvest slightly earlier to get the smaller, egg-sized potatoes, which are best for seed.
- Leave in the light for a week or two to turn green and dormant. Store in egg cartons, somewhere dark and frost-free until spring.

Three to try

1. **'Arran Pilot'** Fine-flavoured new potato
2. **'British Queen'** Reliable, floury second early
3. **'Sarpo Axona'** Blight-resistant maincrop

Growing potatoes in pots

Growing potatoes in repurposed compost sacks or large containers yields a smaller crop, but it's still worth doing. Plant in late winter inside a greenhouse for a super-early crop, or grow specially prepared potatoes through autumn for Christmas.

Tip 30cm (12in) of compost into the sack and bury three first early seed potatoes. Re-bury shoots with more compost as they grow and keep well-watered. When plants flower, your crop should be ready.

Onions and shallots

Once you've mastered traditional onions, get adventurous and try the rest, from sweet red onions and fat shallots to onions that 'walk' around your plot!

SOWING

- Plant overwintering onions in autumn for summer harvests, plus maincrop onions in mid-spring. Shallots need a longer growing season, so plant in early spring.
- Plant sets (immature bulbs) 10–15cm (4–6in) apart, with the tips at the surface.
- Or sow onions from seed, sown direct in mid-spring. Thin seedlings to 10–15cm apart.

CARE

- Keep free of competing weeds and water in prolonged dry spells.

TROUBLESHOOTING

- Remove any flower stems that appear.
- Dry bulbs carefully to avoid neck rot, which is when bulbs rot from the neck down in storage.
- The nasty fungal disease white rot rots bulbs in the ground, so avoid growing onions there again; transfer future crops to containers instead.

HARVESTING

- Lift shallot and onion bulbs after the foliage yellows in midsummer, and dry on racks for a fortnight outside in the sunshine or indoors in a greenhouse or conservatory.
- Once fully dry, plait onions or store in nets somewhere cool and dry.

SAVING SEED

- Leave several good specimens of the same variety in the ground to flower next summer.
- Once seedheads turn brown, snip them off.
- Rub the black seeds loose, remove debris and dry for another week before storing.

Three to try

1. **'Senshyu Yellow'** Super-hardy for autumn sowing
2. **'Stuttgarter'** Handsome flattened bulbs
3. **'Karmen'** Sweet red onions

Spring onions

Sow batches of salad onions monthly from spring to autumn, switching to a winter-hardy variety for your last sowing. Multi-sow under cover, or into drills in the garden or into containers. Harvest young, at 15cm tall.

Perennial onions

Many onions keep coming year after year, so you use a fraction of the resources:

Welsh onions (*Allium fistulosum*) Sow from seed in spring. They grow into clumps, like spring onions, and often stay evergreen. Harvest bulbs and foliage.

Walking onions (*Allium* x *proliferum*) Clusters of mini onions appear halfway up flower stems; pick to eat or let them slowly weigh down the stems to the ground where they root, 'walking' around your plot.

Everlasting onions (*Allium cepa* 'Perutile') Parent bulbs multiply into an ever-widening clump; harvest bulbs as needed, leaving some in the ground to keep producing more.

Annual herbs

Light, summery annual herbs transform your cooking and lift homegrown salads from good to sublime. So, grow lots of them, sowing more each month to pick by the fistful from summer to the first frosts.

FIVE MUST-HAVE HERBS

Basil Warm, spicy flavours, essential for Mediterranean cooking.

- Sow into 5cm (2in) modules indoors from mid-spring.
- Harden off and plant outside in early summer in rich soil and full sun. Basil grows particularly well in greenhouses and in containers.

Chervil Lacy leaves on 60cm (24in) tall stems with a mild aniseed flavour – it's delicious in salads.

- Choose a shady spot for chervil – sow direct into the garden or in containers from mid-spring.
- Sow an extra batch in autumn to pick leaves well into winter.

Coriander Spicy South Asian herb – harvest leaves for salads and seeds for flavouring curries.

- Always sow coriander direct, where it's to grow; from mid-spring, sow along pre-watered drills, or into roomy containers in a sunny spot.
- Pause sowing in summer heat, starting again once the weather cools – late sowings stay leafier for longer.

Dill Tall (90cm; 35in), feathery plants with an aniseed flavour.

- Sow direct from late spring into pre-watered drills in the garden or into containers.
- Harvest leaves young, taking a few from each plant; once flowers appear the harvest ends, so sow several batches through summer.

Summer savory Thyme-like herb, particularly tasty with broad beans.

- Sow in spring into newspaper modules and germinate on a warm windowsill.
- Pot on as they grow, then harden off in early summer and plant outside in free-draining soil in a sunny spot, allowing 20cm (8in) between plants. Savory also grows well in containers.

Perennial herbs

Many summer herbs are perennial, dying back in winter, then regrowing in spring. Though you can sow from seed, you'll start picking sooner if you buy young plants from a peat-free, organic herb supplier (some mail order nurseries also send herbs without the plastic pot).

Mint There's a huge range – grow in containers, as they're invasive in the garden.

Marjoram Spreading, low-growing herb – snip leaves and chop into Mediterranean dishes.

Chives Clump-forming onion relative – both leaves and flowers are edible.

Vegetables to grow in autumn: essential tasks

As the sun falls lower, shadows lengthen and the mellow autumn evenings turn ochre, the summer frenzy slows to a more sedate pace. Autumn vegetables are hearty and comforting – earthy winter squashes, sweet, filling pumpkins and the spicy savouriness of braised chicory. It's time to gather in the last of your harvest and squirrel away your surplus for the winter.

- **Sow green manures** Summer phacelia blankets soil in protective greenery; leave spent stems as winter mulch.
- **Refill greenhouse borders** Transplant winter salads from pots sown in late summer to replace cleared tomatoes and cucumbers.
- **Sow overwintering crops** Broad beans, autumn sown onions and garlic all overwinter well.
- **Clear away plant supports** Pull up canes and hazel rods and store in a shed for next year.
- **Mulch vegetable beds** Spread organic matter 5cm (2in) thick across beds to shield soil from winter weather.
- **Make leaf mould** Collect fallen leaves and stack for fantastic natural soil improver.
- **Lift root crops** Carrots, turnips and parsnips stay tender stored in boxes of damp sand.
- **Stop watering and feeding** As growth slows, water less and stop feeding to help the last fruits ripen.

TIP

Scoop the flesh out of pumpkins, remove seeds, then mix with rice, mince and herbs. Pack it all back into the shell, wrap in foil, roast for 40 minutes and enjoy – the ultimate one-pot meal!

Winter squash

Winter squash and pumpkins grow thicker skins than their summer cousins, and once ripe they act like a protective carapace. So, these are squash you can store, often for a very long time – the best keep for a year or more, as good as the day you picked them.

SOWING

- As for courgettes and summer squash (see page 132).

PLANTING

- Give squash and pumpkins your richest soil and sunniest spot, plus plenty of room – pumpkin plants can reach 2m (7ft) across and more.
- Harden off seedlings in early summer and plant outside at least 1m (3ft) apart.
- Water in well and mulch after planting.

CARE

- Aim to keep the compost damp at all times, but especially when fruiting. Water the base of the plant rather than splashing the leaves, which can cause mildew.

GO GREENER

Winter squashes make a great living mulch – plant alongside tall plants such as sweetcorn and climbing beans, and the broad, spreading leaves suppress weeds and help prevent water evarporation from the soil.

TIP

Keep overenthusiastic stems in bounds by guiding them in a wide circle around the plant as they grow.

Three to try

1. **'Crown Prince'** Large grey fruit
2. **'Potimarron'** Heirloom with rich chestnut flavour
3. **'Jack of All Trades'** Classic Halloween-sized pumpkin

TROUBLESHOOTING

- Mildew is common in late summer. Keep plants well-watered, and spray leaves with a 50:50 mix of milk and water from midsummer to prevent the worst.

HARVESTING

- As fruits deepen in colour in early autumn, lift them onto bricks, so air can circulate.
- Let fruits ripen fully on the plant, then cut them away with 10cm (4in) of stalk still attached.
- Move into a greenhouse or a sunny conservatory to finish drying for another fortnight.
- Store somewhere dry and warm, such as a spare bedroom or greenhouse – place fruits on racks stalk-down so condensation can't collect in the neck and cause rotting.

SAVING SEED

- Follow hand-pollination instructions on page 103.
- Harvest fruit once fully ripe and cure (harden the skins) indoors for another fortnight.
- Cut the fruit in half, scoop out the seeds and wash off any flesh.
- Lay out on a kitchen towel on a sunny windowsill to dry for two weeks.
- Peel seeds off the kitchen towel and store.

Oriental salads

Hardy, cool-season salad greens are invaluable for keeping your salads interesting well into autumn and winter; let them grow to maturity to add unusual umami flavours to stir-fries and miso soup.

SOWING AND GROWING

- Sow only once the weather cools in late summer - Asian salads bolt if it's too hot or dry.
- Choose a spot in part shade, then sow seeds direct into a pre-watered drill.
- If growing to maturity, remove unwanted seedlings to leave the strongest 20–30cm (8–12in) apart.
- Or sow into newspaper modules filled with peat-free compost and place in a cold frame; plant outside once seedlings are 10cm (4in) tall.

TROUBLESHOOTING

- Flea beetles can pepper seedling leaves with holes, but damage is usually minimal this late in the year and plants generally grow through it.

SAVING SEED

- Let just one type of oriental salad set seed, as they cross-pollinate readily.
- Leave in the ground to flower the following spring, then follow instructions as for Brussels sprouts (page 162).

Three to try

1. **Mizuna** Jagged leaves and an umami flavour
2. **Mustard 'Red Frills'** Lacy and mildly peppery
3. **Pak choi** Elegantly waisted hearts

GO GREENER

Plant sweetcorn with dwarf French beans and squash in a classic 'three sisters' combination – the beans provide nitrogen for natural fertilizer, while squash keeps weeds out.

Sweetcorn

Sweetcorn is a late-season treat you'll look forward to all year. They're tall, so give them plenty of room and choose early-maturing varieties to guarantee the plump, sweet cobs ripen fully.

SOWING AND GROWING

- Sow into cardboard toilet roll inners in late spring.
- Harden off seedlings at 10cm (4in) tall and plant outdoors in full sun, in grids with 35–45cm (14–18in) between plants.
- Once tassels turn brown, peel back the outer layer and puncture a kernel. Once you see milky white fluid, twist off the stem and cook right away.

TROUBLESHOOTING

- Birds and mice adore sweetcorn, so cover ripening cobs with cotton bags or tubes of fine wire mesh.

SAVING SEED

- Grow open-pollinated heirloom varieties for seed saving (modern varieties are F1, so not suitable – see page 100).
- Let cobs mature until papery brown, then twist them off, remove the sheath and finish drying somewhere sunny indoors.
- Rub off the kernels and store.

Three to try

1. **'Lark' (F1)** Early, reliable crops
2. **'Golden Bantam'** Heirloom with medium-sweet cobs
3. **'Popcorn'** Multicoloured kernels for popcorn

Garlic

Give garlic plenty of sunshine and it's straightforward to grow. Alongside traditional white bulbs, try gourmet rocambole, porcelain or elephant garlic – you'll be a connoisseur!

SOWING AND GROWING

- Sow in early winter - garlic needs cold weather to form cloves.
- Plant individual cloves, pointy end up, 15cm (6in) apart with tips 2cm (0.8in) below ground level.
- Once leaves die back in summer, lift the crop and dry indoors for a month before plaiting into strings to use as needed.

TROUBLESHOOTING

- Rust can ruin your crop. Fast-maturing hardnecks are less affected. Picking off leaves slows the spread - or grow inside a greenhouse, to keep foliage dry.

SAVING SEED

- Set aside your fattest heads for seed, then simply break apart and plant the cloves.
- Start anew with bought-in stock every few years to avoid diseases building up.

Three to try

1. **'Solent Wight'** Classic white softneck
2. **'Cristo'** Big, pink-tinged bulbs
3. **'Sultop'** Red-skinned hardneck

Hardneck garlic

Hardneck garlics form fewer, fatter cloves than traditional softnecks, with rich, complex flavours. Eat fresh, as they don't store well. Their flower stems, or 'scapes', can be steamed or stir-fried.

TIP

Leave celeriac in the ground until needed, or lift and store in damp sand (see page 99).

Celeriac

Celeriac is autumn comfort food. It tastes just like its close cousin, celery, though it's miles easier to grow; it's especially good mashed with butter, pepper and herbs.

SOWING AND GROWING

- Sow into newspaper modules indoors in early spring, sprinkling seeds onto damp compost without covering, as they need light to germinate.
- Keep seedlings warm, then harden off and plant outside in early summer, 30cm (12in) apart.
- Water generously, never allowing the soil to dry out.
- From early autumn, pull away older leaves to expose the stem and help it swell.

TROUBLESHOOTING

- Plants bolt if seedlings get cold – delay planting outside until the weather warms.
- Celery leaf miner can damage leaves – tolerate minor damage or pick off affected leaves.

SAVING SEED

- Saving seed from celeriac (and celery) is tricky, as seedheads mature erratically and seeds are tiny. If you'd like to have a go, follow the same method as for carrots (see page 140).

Three to try

1. **'Monarch'** Crisp and succulent
2. **'Prinz'** Reliable, with a good flavour
3. **'Giant Prague'** Eastern European heirloom

Chicory and radicchio

Grow traditional chicory to sweeten the mildly bitter flavours by forcing; or grow cabbagey radicchio, which mellows its own scarlet and white hearts inside light-excluding outer leaves.

SOWING AND GROWING

- Sow into pre-watered drills from late spring for baby-leaf salads.
- For heading chicory and radicchio, sow in early summer and thin seedlings to 20–30cm (8–12in) apart.

Forcing chicory

Dig up your biggest plants in late autumn and trim to a 2–3cm (0.8–1in) stump.

Plant upright in damp compost, five to a 25cm (10in) pot, with the crown just above soil level.

Cover with an upturned black pot to exclude light, or keep in a dark cupboard at 10°C (50°F).

Harvest the pale-yellow sprouts (chicons) at 15cm (6in); cover the pot again and they'll resprout.

TROUBLESHOOTING

- Chicory bolts if it's too dry, so keep it well-watered.

SAVING SEED

- Leave just one variety in the ground to flower the following summer.
- Mash seedheads with a rolling pin to extract the hard-to-remove seeds, then thresh and winnow (see page 102).

Three to try

1. **Radicchio 'Palla Rossa'** Flame-red and white heads
2. **Chicory 'Witloof'** Classic forcing variety
3. **Chicory 'Pain de Sucre'** Mild and lettuce-like

GO GREENER

Make good use of every part of your crop – hefty winter radish leaves also make great spinachy greens, and the flowers and crisp green seedpods are delicious, too.

Oriental radish (mooli)

Winter radishes are as ridiculously easy to grow as their summer cousins, but make hefty, mild-flavoured roots, at their best cooked into stir-fries and stews or fermented to make traditional kimchi.

SOWING AND GROWING

- Sow direct into pre-watered drills in late summer.
- Thin seedlings to 15–20cm (6–8in) apart.
- Lift roots at 10–20cm (4–8in) long from late autumn.

TROUBLESHOOTING

- Roots fail to swell and sometimes split if they're too dry or overcrowded, so give plants plenty of room and water in dry spells.

SAVING SEED

- Leave several of your best roots in the ground to flower the following year.
- Once seedpods turn brown and dry, harvest and bring indoors.
- Place in a bag and crush with a rolling pin to release the seeds. Winnow out the debris (see page 102) and store.

Three to try

1. **'Neptune'** Classic long, white mooli radish
2. **'Black Spanish'** Round with a black skin
3. **'Watermelon'** Heirloom with white skins and scarlet hearts

Vegetables to grow in winter: essential tasks

It may be tempting to retreat inside as the weather cools, but when you're harvesting from your plot year-round, the vegetable patch still needs tending – and there's no better excuse to wrap up warm and make the most of those crisp, blue-sky winter days.

- **Support tall brassicas** Drive stakes in alongside top-heavy sprouts, kale and purple sprouting broccoli and tie in securely.
- **Turn the compost** Fork compost out of the bin, then back in again to blend ingredients, then cover with cardboard against winter wet.
- **Hoe annual weeds** In warmer winters, annual weeds keep growing – so hoe monthly.
- **Prune fruit trees** Sharpen those secateurs – winter is prime pruning time for fruit trees (except stone fruit such as cherries) and soft fruit, too.
- **Plant bare-root fruit** Buying bare root in winter avoids peat-based compost and plastic pots, plus they're dormant, so settle in better.
- **Protect salad crops** Pop glass cloches over salads to prevent leaves getting unappetizingly shredded in winter gales.
- **Pick off yellowing leaves** Brassicas shed leaves naturally, but yellowing foliage harbours pests and fungal diseases such as botrytis, so pick off regularly.
- **Get ready for spring** On stormy days when you can't get outside, start dreaming up next season: new crops, new techniques, extra garden space… spring will be here soon!

Sprouts

Brussels sprouts and closely related kalettes are iconic winter crops and are straightforward to grow, but they're large, slow-growing plants, so give them plenty of space and a long growing season.

SOWING

- Sow in mid-spring – you won't need many (roughly 10 plants feed a family of four generously), so scatter seeds over homemade or peat-free multipurpose compost in 10cm (4in) clay pots.
- Or sow direct outside into drills in a finely raked seedbed in your sunniest corner. Remove the smallest seedlings to leave the strongest 5cm (2in) apart.

PLANTING

- Once seedlings are about 10cm tall, plant outside into rich soil in a sunny spot, leaving 60cm (24in) between plants.
- Plant deeply, so the lowest leaves are just above soil level.
- Firm in very well, and water.

CARE

- Water through dry spells.
- Remove yellowing leaves regularly to avoid fungal disease.
- Stake plants firmly in autumn against winter gales.

TROUBLESHOOTING

- In acidic soil, add calcified seaweed three months before planting out.

- Cabbage white caterpillars and pigeons can be devastating, so grow under mesh cages from the start.

HARVESTING

- Cut off the cabbagey tops in late autumn to enjoy as an extra harvest.
- Pick sprouts from bottom to top, snapping them away from the stem when tightly closed and about the size of a walnut.

SAVING SEED

- Save from only one type of brassica flower each season, to avoid cross-pollination.
- In spring, allow about 12 of your best plants to flower for good genetic diversity.
- Once seed pods turn brown, cut the whole head to dry indoors.

GO GREENER

Instead of plastic insect-proof mesh, butterfly- and pigeon-proof your sprouts with cages of PLA (plastic-free cornstarch) insect-proof mesh or, even better, second-hand cotton bedsheets or muslin.

Three to try

1. **'Falstaff'** Deliciously nutty purple sprouts
2. **'Evesham Special'** Reliable early variety
3. **'Trafalgar'** Traditional Christmas cropper

GO GREENER

There's no need to pull up your cabbages after harvesting; leave stumps in the ground and they'll resprout with leafy shoots to pick and eat.

Savoy cabbages

One of the most handsome of all cabbages, with dark green, usually deeply crinkled leaves and a lovely rich flavour, savoys are hardy enough to withstand ice and snow.

SOWING AND GROWING

- Sow in late spring - sprinkle seed onto peat-free multipurpose compost in a 10cm (4in) pot, or into newspaper modules or soil blocks (see page 48).
- Or sow into a well-prepared seedbed outdoors, removing weaker seedlings to leave the strongest to grow 5cm (2in) apart.
- Transplant young plants outside at 10cm tall, with the lowest leaves just above soil level.

TROUBLESHOOTING

- Grow under mesh cages from the start to fend off caterpillars and pigeons.
- Place felt collars around the base of stems to prevent cabbage root fly laying eggs.
- In acidic soil, add calcified seaweed three months before planting out.

SAVING SEED

- As for spring cabbage (see page 121).

Three to try

1. **'January King'** Purple-tinged, relatively smooth leaves
2. **'Vertus'** Deep green and crinkly
3. **'Tourmaline'** Reliable and disease resistant

Parsnips

Long, tapering parsnips are slow-growing, trouble-free roots. Leave them in the ground through winter and harvest as needed – roast or mash with carrots to enjoy their hearty, warming winter flavour.

SOWING AND GROWING

- Sow direct outside. Make a shallow drill 1-2cm (0.5in) deep and water first so the soil is damp, then space seeds along the bottom about 5cm (2in) apart before lightly covering with more soil.
- Parsnip seeds germinate very slowly - sprinkle fast-growing radish seeds into the drill, too, to mark the row and give you an extra crop.

TROUBLESHOOTING

- Parsnips fork in stony or over-rich soil. Avoid manure or fertilizers, and in stony soils make a hole with a crowbar, fill with 50:50 sand and sieved soil and sow into that.
- Canker can cause rotting - choose resistant varieties and wait until mid-spring before sowing.

SAVING SEED

- Leave several of your best plants in the ground after winter.
- Flower spikes appear in early summer - they're very tall and may need staking.
- Once the seeds turn brown, cut the whole head and shake out seeds.

Three to try

1. **'White Spear'** Short, chunky roots
2. **'Avonresister'** Canker resistant
3. **'Tender and True'** Traditional long roots

GO GREENER

When thinning seedlings, save those that you remove – dig them up carefully and transplant them to make another row of vegetables.

Leeks

A must-have for the winter plot, leeks are incredibly hardy and can stay in the ground until you're ready to harvest.

SOWING AND GROWING

- Sow from early spring into newspaper modules filled with peat-free seed compost. Water, then sow a few seeds on top and cover with more compost. Thin to one seedling for fewer, larger leeks, or leave three or four seedlings for a clump.
- Transplant outside at 10–15cm (4–6in) tall, 15cm apart. Make a hole 15cm deep, drop in a seedling, then fill the hole with water – no need to backfill with soil.
- Or sow direct outside – make shallow channels, water, then scatter seeds along the bottom. Cover lightly with more soil.

TROUBLESHOOTING

- Grow under cages of PLA (plastic-free cornstarch) insect-proof mesh or second-hand cotton bedsheets to avoid leek moth and alium leaf miner.
- Remove leaves affected by rust.
- Pinch out any developing flower stalks (they're edible!).

SAVING SEED

- As for onions (see page 146).

Three to try

1. **'Musselburgh'** Sturdy white shanks
2. **'Bleu de Solaise'** Gorgeous slate-blue leaves
3. **'King Richard'** For summer baby leeks

Parsley (moss curled)

You can have fresh, richly flavoured parsley to pick almost year-round: fine-flavoured flat-leaved parsley sown in spring makes good summer picking, then in midsummer, sow super-hardy moss curled parsley to stay green outside all winter.

SOWING AND GROWING

- Sow under cover into newspaper modules – fill with seed compost, then sow a few seeds into each, cover with compost and water. Once germinated, remove all but the largest seedling in each module to grow on. Transplant outside, 10cm apart, once 8–10cm (3–4in) tall.
- Or sow direct into the garden – make a shallow channel 1–2cm (0.5–1in) deep with a trowel, then sprinkle seed along the bottom about 1cm apart. Cover lightly with more soil.
- Grows well in containers – sow direct onto compost, then thin seedlings to 3–5cm (1–2in) apart.
- Parsley seed takes up to a month to germinate, so be patient.

TROUBLESHOOTING

- Parsley can bolt if it's too hot or dry, so give it a damp spot in partial shade.

SAVING SEED

- As for parsnips (see page 165).

Three to try

1. **'Moss Curled'** For winter harvesting
2. **var. *neapolitanum*** Flat-leaved Italian summer variety
3. **var. *tuberosum*** Hamburg parsley that also gives parsnip-like roots

Charts and planners

Sample square foot plan

Dividing your vegetable plot into small sections, planting one crop per square foot, allows you to grow a great variety of plants in one place. For more detail, see page 27.

COURGETTE 'Patio Star' 1 plant 	**LETTUCE** 'Salad Bowl' 4 plants 	**FRENCH BEAN** 'Cobra' 2 plants 	**FRENCH BEAN** 'Cobra' 2 plants 
BEETROOT 'Bolthardy' 9 plants 	**LEEK** 'King Richard' 9 plants 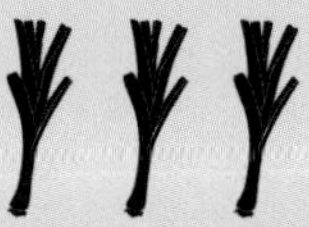	**FRENCH BEAN** 'Cobra' 2 plants 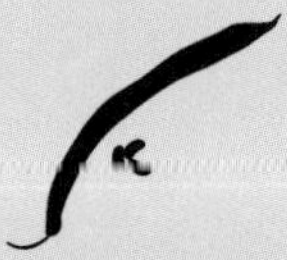	**FRENCH BEAN** 'Cobra' 2 plants 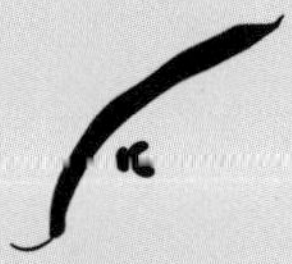
CARROT 'Market Atlas' 16 plants 	**CALABRESE** 'Matsuri' 1 plant 	**SALAD ROCKET** 'Broadcast sown' 	**SWISS CHARD** 'Patio Star' 1 plant 
BUSH TOMATO 'Losetto' 1 plant 	**COURGETTE** 'Patio Star' 1 plant 	**TURNIP** 'Tokyo Cross' 1 plant 	**NASTURTIUM** 'Empress of India' 1 plant 

Sowing and planting table

Try combining some of these crops to keep your vegetable beds full for as much of the year as possible

Sow

Harvest

Vegetable	JAN	FEB	MAR	APR	MAY	JUN	JUL	AUG	SEP	OCT	NOV	DEC
Potatoes		Sow	Sow	Sow		Harvest	Harvest	Harvest	Harvest			
Broad beans		Sow	Sow	Sow	Harvest	Harvest	Harvest	Harvest		Sow	Sow	
Carrots		Sow	Sow	Sow	Sow	Sow / Harvest	Sow / Harvest	Harvest	Harvest	Harvest		
Beetroot		Sow	Sow	Sow / Harvest	Sow / Harvest	Sow / Harvest	Sow / Harvest	Sow / Harvest	Harvest	Harvest		
Spring cabbage		Harvest	Harvest	Harvest			Sow	Sow				
Sweetcorn				Sow	Sow		Harvest	Harvest				
Squash					Sow	Sow	Harvest	Harvest	Harvest	Harvest		
Leeks	Harvest		Sow	Sow					Harvest	Harvest	Harvest	Harvest
Tomatoes		Sow	Sow			Harvest	Harvest	Harvest				
French beans				Sow	Sow	Sow	Harvest	Harvest	Harvest	Harvest		
Courgettes				Sow			Harvest	Harvest	Harvest			
Oriental salads					Sow	Sow	Harvest	Harvest	Harvest	Harvest	Harvest	
Chicory						Sow	Sow		Harvest	Harvest		
Moss-curled parsley	Harvest	Sow / Harvest	Sow / Harvest	Sow / Harvest	Sow / Harvest	Sow / Harvest	Sow / Harvest	Sow / Harvest	Harvest	Harvest	Harvest	Harvest
Garlic	Sow					Harvest	Harvest			Sow	Sow	Sow
Onions (from sets Sep–Nov) (from seeds Dec–Feb)	Sow	Sow				Harvest	Harvest		Sow	Sow	Sow	
Celeriac		Sow	Sow	Sow	Sow					Harvest	Harvest	Harvest

Further reading

Back Garden Seed Saving
Sue Stickland
Eco-Logic Books, 2008

RHS Can I Grow Potatoes in Pots?
Sally Nex
Mitchell Beazley, 2022

Growing Self Sufficiency
Sally Nex
Green Books, 2017

RHS Grow Your Own Crops in Pots
Kay Maguire
Mitchell Beazley, 2022

RHS How Can I Help Hedgehogs?
Helen Bostock and Sophie Collins
Mitchell Beazley, 2019

How to Grow Perennial Vegetables
Martin Crawford
Green Books, 2012

RHS How to Grow Plants from Seeds
Sophie Collins
Mitchell Beazley, 2021

How to Grow the Low-carbon Way
Sally Nex
DK, 2021

RHS Resilient Garden
Tom Massey
DK, 2023

RHS Step-by-Step Veg Patch
Lucy Chamberlain
DK, 2020

The Garden Jungle
Prof. Dave Goulson
Vintage, 2020

The Vegetable Gardener's Guide to Permaculture
Christopher Shein & Julie Thompson
Timber Press, 2013

Wild about Weeds
Jack Wallington
Laurence King, 2019

Grow Food for Free
Huw Richards
DK, 2020

WEB RESOURCES

Charles Dowding's No Dig Gardening charlesdowding.co.uk

Garden Organic gardenorganic.org.uk

Permaculture Association permaculture.org.uk

Royal Horticultural Society rhs.org.uk

Soil blocker machinery soilblockers.co.uk

Index

PICTURE CREDITS

Guide: TL Top left, ML Middle left BL Bottom left, TR Top right, MR Middle Right BR Bottom right

2 GAP Photos/Graham Strong, 5 Arco / O. Diez / Imagebroker / Alamy Stock Photo, 6-7 Linda George/Shutterstock, 8 Morinka/Shutterstock, 9 cjp/iStockphoto, 10-11 sanjeri/iStockphoto, 12 GAP Photos/Fiona Lea, 14 All GAP Photos/Howard Rice, 15 GAP Photos/Nicola Stocken, 15 bottom Kolonko/Shutterstock, 17 Gordon Swanson/Shutterstock, 18 Phill Thornton Photo/Shutterstock, 19 GAP Photos - Becky Westover, 22 left GAP Photos, 22 right GAP Photos/Joanna Kossak - Gabriel Ash, 23 top Tim Gainey / Alamy Stock Photo, 23 BL GAP Photos/Torie Chugg, 23 BR Clare Gainey / Alamy Stock Photo, 24 Paul Maguire/Shutterstock, 25 TL mtreasure/iStockphoto, 25 ML GAP Photos/Christa Brand - Elke Zimmermann, 25 BL GAP Photos/Juliette Wade, 25 TR GAP Photos/Graham Strong, 26 kovaciclea/iStockphoto, 27 TL GAP Photos/Leigh Clapp - Design: Tom Massey, 27 TR GAP Photos/Stephen Studd - Designer: Professor Nigel Dunnett, 27 BR GAP Photos/ Maxine Adcock, 28 GAP Photos/Robert Mabic, 29 TL Mabuka/Shutterstock, 29 TR Paul Maguire/Shutterstock, 29 MR Ryoko Fujiwara/Shutterstock, 29 BR Jullex51/Shutterstock, 30 GAP Photos/Lynn Keddie, 32 Halfpoint/Shutterstock, 33 TL nednapa/Shutterstock, 33 ML GAP Photos/John Glover, 33 ML Victoria_Hunter/Shutterstock, 33 BL Ulada/Shutterstock, 33 TR Natallia Ploskaya/Shutterstock, 34 sophiecat/Shutterstock, 35 Peter Turner Photography/Shutterstock, 36 CasarsaGuru/ iStockphoto, 37 TL CLICKMANIS/Shutterstock, 37 ML darksoul72/Shutterstock, 37 ML Alexander Tolstykh/Shutterstock, 37 BL romiri/Shutterstock, 37 TR tomertu/Shutterstock, 38 GAP Photos, 39 GAP Photos/Michael King, 40 reflexion I nature/ Shutterstock, 41 TL barmalini/Shutterstock, 41 ML nnattalli/Shutterstock, 41 ML iMarzi/Shutterstock, 41 BL Niliane Fatima Pierok/Shutterstock, 41 TR tamu1500/Shutterstock, 42 left FooTToo/Shutterstock, 42 right blessingscaptured/Shutterstock, 43 GAP Photos/Anna Omiotek-Tott - Designed by Gabrielle Evans, 44-45 GAP Photos/Robert Mabic, 46 top GAP Photos/Elke Borkowski, 46 bottom Vaivirga/iStockphoto, 47 top GAP Photos/Maxine Adcock, 47 bottom Zbynek Pospisil/iStockphoto, 50 TL EvgeniusD/Shutterstock, 50 BL Sally Nex, 50 TR GAP Photos, 51 top GAP Photos/Tim Gainey, 51 bottom GAP Photos/ Christa Brand, 55 TL Ashley-Belle Burns/Shutterstock, 55 BL A Kisel/Shutterstock, 55 TR Gennadiy Kravchenko/iStockphoto, 57 GAP Photos/Dave Bevan, 58 FotoHelin/Shutterstock, 59 top beekeepx/iStockphoto, 59 bottom Matt_Brown/iStockphoto, 60 JoeDunckley/iStockphoto, 61 top GAP Photos/Michael Howes, 61 bottom GAP Photos/Anna Omiotek-Tott - Designers: Helen J Rosevear and Jane Stoneham, 62 GAP Photos/Robert Mabic, 63 TL Nicky Rhodes/Shutterstock, 63 ML Konmac/Shutterstock, 63 BL Lia_Russy/Shutterstock, 63 TR filippo giuliani/Shutterstock, 63 MR Igor Paszkiewicz/Shutterstock, 63 BR Przemyslaw Muszynski/Shutterstock, 65 Marcus Lindstrom/iStockphoto, 66 & 67 left GAP Photos/John Glover, 67 middle olgadiukareva/ Shutterstock, 67 right S.O.E/Shutterstock, 68 top GAP Photos/Jonathan Buckley, 68 bottom Deborah Vernon / Alamy Stock Photo, 69 GAP Photos/Pernilla Bergdahl - Design: del Buono Gazerwitz, 70 Vasilii Kosarev/Shutterstock, 71 Andi111/ Shutterstock, 72 GAP Photos/Jonathan Buckley, 75 top (clockwise 1-5) Jirik V/Shutterstock, Janis Smits/Shutterstock, nnattalli/ Shutterstock, INTREEGUE Photography/Shutterstock, sophiecat/Shutterstock, 75 bottom (clockwise 1-5) Kanjanee Chaisin/ Shutterstock, Ruta Saulyte-Laurinaviciene/Shutterstock, Nadia Nice/Shutterstock, husnainshafiq/Shutterstock, Deyan Georgiev/ Shutterstock, 76 Mooi Design/Shutterstock, 77 GAP Photos/Tim Gainey, 78 GAP Photos/Dave Bevan, 79 Jane Tansi, 80 GAP Photos/Howard Rice - Design: Terry Lynch, 81 Elizabeth Whiting & Associates / Alamy Stock Photo, 82 JulieK2/Shutterstock, 83 top Patrick Daxenbichler/Shutterstock, 83 middle Anna Yakymenko/Shutterstock, 83 bottom OMfotovideocontent/ Shutterstock, 84 Paul Maguire/Shutterstock, 85 D. Kucharski K. Kucharska/Shutterstock, 85 Korostylev Dmitrii/Shutterstock, 86 David Prahl/Shutterstock, 87 TL LFRabanedo/Shutterstock, 87 ML Mr. Meijer/Shutterstock, 87 ML Montypeter/Shutterstock, 87 BL guppyss/Shutterstock, 87 right Flower_Garden/Shutterstock, 88 cjp/iStockphoto, 89 top bgwalker/iStockphoto, 89 bottom Alec Issigonis/Shutterstock, 90 GAP Photos/Nicola Stocken, 91 GAP Photos/Gary Smith, 92 GAP Photos/Jacqui Hurst - Designer: Carol Klein, 93 Carolina Jaramillo/Shutterstock, 94 GAP Photos/Sarah Cuttle, 95 GAP Photos/John Glover, 96 1715d1db_3/iStockphoto, 97 top Irina Malyutina/iStockphoto, 97 bottom Irina Malyutina/iStockphoto, 98 Irina Malyutina/iStockphoto, 99 TL GAP Photos/Jonathan Buckley, 99 TR Grusho Anna/Shutterstock, 99 BR HandmadePictures/ Shutterstock, 101 TL gardeningpix / Alamy Stock Photo, 101 TR khudoliy/iStockphoto, 101 bottom Graham Corney/ Shutterstock, 102 CasarsaGuru/iStockphoto, 103 TL Denis Pogostin/Shutterstock, 103 TR Pattakorn Uttarasak/Shutterstock, 103 BR Dorling Kindersley ltd / Alamy Stock Photo, 104-105 alicja neumiler/Shutterstock, 106 top Moyo Studio/iStockphoto, 106 bottom rukawajung/Shutterstock, 107 Valentina_G/Shutterstock, 108 Martien van Gaalen/Shutterstock, 109 Geo-grafika/ Shutterstock, 110 Alexander Tolstykh/Shutterstock, 111 Victoria_Hunter/Shutterstock, 112 Aprilphoto/Shutterstock, 113 Julia Senkevich/Shutterstock, 114 nnattalli/Shutterstock, 115 Yolanta/Shutterstock, 116 iMarzi/Shutterstock, 117 Danny Hummel/Shutterstock, 118 top Foxxy63/Shutterstock, 118 bottom Mike_shots/Shutterstock, 119 GAP Photos/Carole Drake, 120 New Africa/Shutterstock, 121 sunakri/Shutterstock, 122 Linda George/Shutterstock, 123 marcin jucha/Shutterstock, 124 top yizhachok/Shutterstock, 124 bottom Uryupina Nadezhda/Shutterstock, 125 alicja neumiler/Shutterstock, 126 vaivirga/ Shutterstock, 127 Vlad Siaber/Shutterstock, 128 Peter Turner Photography/Shutterstock, 129 barmalini/Shutterstock, 130 Peter Turner Photography/Shutterstock, 131 CTatiana/Shutterstock, 132 Diane N. Ennis/Shutterstock, 133 i-am-helen/Shutterstock, 134 nnattalli/Shutterstock, 135 Caron Badkin/Shutterstock, 136 sadecestock/Shutterstock, 137 PHILIPPE MONTIGNY/ Shutterstock, 138 Duqie/Shutterstock, 139 Peter Turner Photography/Shutterstock, 140 Kati Finell/Shutterstock, 141 New Africa/Shutterstock, 142 Olga Bondarenko/Shutterstock, 143 Nadia Nice/Shutterstock, 144 Tricky_Shark/Shutterstock, 145 Photos Horticultural / Avalon.red / Alamy Stock Photo, 146 left Art_Pictures/Shutterstock, 146 middle bluejava1/Shutterstock, 147 Shebeko/Shutterstock, 148 JoannaTkaczuk/Shutterstock, 149 tm_photografie/Shutterstock, 150 fotografixx/iStockphoto, 151 Yotka/Shutterstock, 152 Peter Turner Photography/Shutterstock, 153 Yann Avril / BIOSPHOTO / Alamy Stock Photo, 154 Cecilia Di Dio/Shutterstock, 155 Fajar Tri Amboro/Shutterstock, 156 Denis Pogostin/Shutterstock, 157 Andrew Fletcher/ Shutterstock, 158 Dani Vincek/Shutterstock, 159 Gregory Johnston/Shutterstock, 160 top Ihor Hvozdetskyi/Shutterstock, 160 bottom M G White/Shutterstock, 161 pcturner71/iStockphoto, 162 lucentius/iStockphoto, 163 mm7/Shutterstock, 164 viki2win/Shutterstock, 165 Zbynek Pospisil/iStockphoto, 166 yuris/Shutterstock, 167 tm_photografie/Shutterstock

Every effort has been made to credit the copyright holders of the images used in these books. We apologise for any unintentional omissions or errors and will insert the appropriate acknowledgements to any companies or individuals in subsequent editions of the work